D1743899

YOU WERE BORN INVINCIBLE

OVERCOME ANY OBSTACLE
SOLVE ANY PROBLEM
ACHIEVE ANY GOAL

BY

T.D. MCKENZIE

You Were Born Invincible

By T.D. McKenzie

Publisher:
McKenzie Training
PO Box 88
Harrow
Middlesex
London
United Kingdom
HA2 0WL

ISBN 0-9548166-1-7
First edition.

For Leroy

Table of Contents

ACKNOWLEDGEMENTS

Special Thanks

As I reflect on the completion of this book, I am moved to thank the many people who have touched my life and inspired me to write it; many are friends and family members, while others are simply those special individuals whose writings and examples have been beacons of light for me throughout the years.

My heartfelt thanks to you all.

Delroy Braham, Sean Braham, Jay Braham, Carmen McKenzie, Kenric McKenzie, Colin McKenzie, Lester McKenzie, Florrie Leo, Sean Leo, Patricia Leo, Gonzague Leo, Melissa Leo, Kennie Leo, Marcus Leo, Kester Leo, Lynne Leo, Neville Clarke, Tahera Hussein, Delores Fearon, Hale Dwoskin, Anna Benjamin, Warren Benjamin, Paulette Ludford, Nadine McLeod, Derek Powell, Veronica Powell, José Silva, Deepak Chopra, Bill Phillips, Dan Millman, Wayne W. Dyer, Bob Scheinfeld, Stan Lee, Lester Levenson and Bill Cosby.

I would also like to thank two of the most amazing people I know, my Mum and Dad, who have showed me what it truly means to be invincible in the face of adversity.

A special note of appreciation goes out to a wonderful woman who has demonstrated total and complete faith in me from the very beginning of this project, my beautiful wife Marian.

Finally, I would like to thank God for guiding me on this long and often difficult journey and for the many gifts I have received as a result.

INTRODUCTION

How This Book Came to Be

One of my earliest childhood memories is of sitting on the edge of my mother's bed, totally absorbed in the Superman cartoon that played every morning during the summer months.

I can't recall exactly what time it started, but as soon as I heard the introduction I was hooked.

"Faster than a speeding bullet, more powerful than a locomotive, able to leap tall buildings in a single bound. Look, up in the sky! It's a bird; it's a plane; it's Superman!"

Every time I heard those words it was a signal to me that a new adventure was about to start, and somehow, no matter what I was doing, I always found myself perched in my favourite spot in front of the TV.

I feel no shame in saying I was fascinated by Superman; after all, he is a man who can fly, rescue people from danger, avert disasters, and still find time for a day job.

I even considered becoming a superhero myself, but after my failed attempt at lifting my parents' bed I realised it was not a viable option. However, this never stopped me from being fascinated by Superman, and as I got older my interest spread to other comic book superheroes.

In addition to Superman, I became a fan of other heroes such as Batman, Spiderman, and the X-Men. Regardless of what was happening in my life and the many challenges I faced during those years as a young man growing up in London, comics became a refuge in which I could lose myself.

As I moved into my late teens, my curiosity shifted from comic fantasy to personal growth and self-help. After being exposed to the world of costumed heroes endowed with special abilities, I became intensely curious about the hidden potential of human beings in the real world.

I was also in need of answers to issues within my own life, as I had begun to experience periods of depression and hopelessness soon after I left school. This resulted in a period of isolation and despair, which lasted until I made a little discovery.

When I was around seventeen I came across a book called The Power of Self-Hypnosis, advertised in my local free ads paper and available via mail order. The claims it made about being able to transform lives by tapping the power of the unconscious mind seemed almost too good to be true. I quickly ordered a copy anyway.

The reading of this book was to mark a pivotal point in my life, as it was my introduction to the human potential movement, as it was then known, and kick-started a journey of personal discovery.

Since that time I have read and studied over six hundred books relating to the subject of personal development, covering areas such as Neuro Linguistic Programming, Emotional Releasing, Accelerated Learning, Self-Healing, and Creative Visualisation. I have also listened to well over one hundred audio programs, as well as attended numerous workshops and seminars.

As a result of this period of study I am now a professional coach and trainer specialising in personal change strategies.

The book you now have in your possession is the culmination of a year's work, which I completed during a particularly difficult period in my life.

It began with a question one afternoon, when I started to wonder about the underlying principles behind many of the tools I had mastered over the years.

That question was:

What is the number one key to achieving phenomenal success?

This self-inquiry sparked another question:

What is the vital component behind every technique for personal change I have ever learned?

For the better part of three months I became obsessed with finding the answers to these two questions, and was spurred on to study the fundamental principles of a wide variety of tools and strategies.

This period of research, which began in December 2002, resulted in two phenomenal discoveries.

For years I had searched for the secrets to creating a life of wealth and happiness, the timeless principles that would allow me to live the life of my dreams. Turns out the truth had been staring me in the face all along!

My First Discovery

There is only one factor that guarantees your success in life.

Every self-help book or program uses it in some way, but most of the time its importance is simply overlooked.

Success has nothing to do with your education, intelligence, gender, age, race, or class. It has nothing to do with luck, fate, destiny, or even whether you are a morally upstanding person.

So what's the secret? What is it that truly separates the super successful and the phenomenally wealthy from the rest of the population?

I'll tell you in one simple word: **beliefs.**

The beliefs we hold about ourselves and the world we live in make up the primary force that dictates the course of our lives.

It is our beliefs that determine how much money we earn, whom we marry, the hobbies we enjoy, the friends we have, and even...when we will die.

This is the force that has been working behind the scenes to create many of your successes and failures. It is incredibly powerful, yet at the same time totally of your own making.

It doesn't matter if you study books such as The Seven Spiritual Laws of Success, How to Manifest Your Destiny, The Power of Positive Thinking or tap yourself on the head three times while reciting a mystical chant – if you believe with every fibre of your being that it will be effective, then your success will follow.

On the other hand, if you believe that "No matter what strategy or technique I learn, it never yields any positive results," then you will be proved right regardless of the effectiveness of the tools you use.

So if our beliefs are the key, how can we harness their immense power and use them to our advantage?

My Second Discovery

Inspired by a passage from the Bible, I discovered that by employing a unique process of questioning a person could access the untapped resources of the mind, including the ability to permanently erase limiting beliefs.

This breakthrough allowed me to create an incredibly powerful system that will allow you to transform virtually every aspect of your life.

Much of what you will learn in this manual forms part of a two-day course I have created called **The McKenzie Mastery Process™**.

I have taken the key principles from this program to provide you with a complete home study course you can learn at your own pace.

What Can You Expect?

One of the issues I have noted as a long-time avid reader of personal growth material is the huge amount of irrelevant and unnecessary information that is included in many books, which does nothing to advance the readers' understanding or grasp of the key ideas.

I have often waded through two hundred to five hundred pages of material, only to discover that it wasn't relevant to the problem I wanted to solve.

When I decided to develop this material for publication, I promised myself I would avoid this tendency and spare my readers the agony of ploughing through page after page of useless information before finally getting to the point.

This is why I have adopted the format of a manual rather than your usual self-help book layout. You will not find in these pages a lengthy history of the tools and strategies espoused, nor will you find a parade of unnecessary illustrations and charts.

I have included just the information you need to apply the techniques to your life and make the changes you desire.

The manual is split into two sections, each one covering a specific aspect of the program.

Section One

This section provides a basic understanding of how you came to be the person you are today and gives a brief overview of what has been holding you back from living the life of your dreams.

Section Two

Here we launch straight into the powerful tools that will allow you to make rapid changes in your personal and professional lives. This section includes step-by-step instructions of the techniques, together with practice sessions.

By the time you have read and completed all the exercises in this material you will be able to:

- Program your mind to achieve any goal
- Find the solution to any problem
- Permanently erase limiting beliefs
- Improve any relationship, past or present
- Access deep states of inner peace, relaxation, and happiness
- Heal deeply painful emotional issues

All of the above and more will be yours if you follow the simple steps as directed. Do not be concerned as to whether you will be able to grasp and understand the techniques that follow, as I have taught them to people ranging from ten to sixty years of age.

How to Use This Manual

The best way to approach this material is simply to read sections one and two from start to finish and complete the exercises as directed.

Once you have read through the manual, simply return to those techniques that offer solutions to your most pressing problems and begin working on them.

What's Required of You

To fully use the unique tools within this manual, all that I require from you are:

- An open mind
- A notepad and pen to make notes
- A promise that you will complete the practice sessions as and when directed

That's it! That is all you need to grasp the life changing information this material offers.

So, will the techniques in this manual allow you to leap tall buildings in a single bound? Not exactly, but I can guarantee one thing: after applying these simple tools to the issues and challenges you face in your daily life, you will experience a newfound resilience and will become virtually **invincible** in the pursuit of your goals.

If you are ready to make the ultimate breakthrough in your life and change the course of your destiny, get ready for a powerful transformational experience!

Best of success,
T.D. McKenzie

CHAPTER

ONE

The Forces That Shape Us

Our present circumstances are the fruits of our past experience.

Your School of Conditioning

In many ways the person you are today is the result of the continuous conditioning you have experienced since birth.

What this involved was an intensive daily education of how to be a human being. Your parents or caregivers are the people mainly responsible for this, from the moment you were born all the way through your childhood.

This conditioning continues even into adulthood; however, the media and other authority figures may (as usually happens) take over this role.

What you learn during this important phase of your life is how to survive in this strange place called planet earth.

You learn that you are of a particular gender, race, and culture; you also develop your likes and dislikes, with your own personal view of the world, better known as your belief system.

Depending on the parenting skills your caregivers possess at the time, you either grow up to be a confident, successful individual who positively contributes to society, or an emotionally damaged person who becomes - as often happens - the source of some of society's problems.

An Interesting Fact about Elephants

In many parts of India, elephants are used for manual labour; it is a tradition that has been a part of their culture for thousands of years.

Now although they are relatively peaceful animals, elephants are incredibly strong and can be difficult to control, as they can weigh eight thousand pounds or more once fully grown.

To deal with this, handlers developed a method that allows them to "condition" elephants while they are still young.

This conditioning involves tying a young elephant's legs to a stake in the ground with a very thick rope, which prevents it from moving more than a few feet.

Whenever the baby elephant attempts to break free, it discovers that the rope is too strong. Although the elephant may attempt several times to escape, over time it eventually gives up and accepts its fate.

As the elephant grows to its full size, it continues to accept the idea that the rope prevents it from being free, even when the strong rope is replaced with a flimsier version.

With this belief firmly in place, the handlers can restrain a full-sized elephant easily with very small ropes and little supervision.

Now, it is easy to see that elephants and human beings are completely different; however, this story shows how conditioning can keep an animal clearly superior to humans in strength and size under control.

The reality of this example is that the elephant can walk away at any time, and that it would be pretty difficult for its handlers to stop it if it chose to do so. It is its belief system that tells it walking away is impossible, and so it stays captive for the rest of its life.

No, we are not elephants, but just like the elephant, many of us create limiting beliefs about ourselves and the world at a young age. We base them on mostly inaccurate information, and it is these beliefs that are the cause of many of our present problems.

The Pivotal Years

Many psychologists agree that the most crucial time in human development is the period between birth and age five. During this phase we form the specific character traits and attitudes we carry into adulthood.

Throughout this period we begin to recognise the world around us and start an epic learning process. We learn that we have bodies that need feeding and that we are dependent on adults for all our comfort and security.

During this phase of our development we learn at an incredible rate; we are sponges soaking up new experiences. We are intensely curious about our surroundings and constantly test the boundaries of our new world.

One drawback at this early stage of our lives is that we take everything around us literally. Much of what we are told by our parents, teachers, and other authority figures is often misinterpreted because we have not yet developed the ability and gained the life experiences to test the validity of certain statements or beliefs.

If someone we trust tells us something about the world or ourselves while we are in this early stage of growth, we often accept it as truth.

It is these concepts that create many of the attitudes, prejudices and fears we struggle with in later life.

Punishment and Reward

Throughout much of childhood we are controlled through a process of punishment and reward. If we do something to please our parents or other authority figures we receive a reward in the form of affection or treats.

However, if we do something that displeases them we are often disciplined, which may involve the withholding of affection, limitation of freedom, and in some cases, physical punishment.

As a result of this process, we learn to link pleasure to pleasing others and pain to doing the opposite. This constant need for approval is one of the many causes of the stress and unhappiness now so widespread in modern society.

From our childlike perspective, we link saying "no" to others with disapproval and a possible threat to our survival, and as a result we learn to change our behaviour to avoid this.

This early model of behaviour forms the basis of all our future relationships, which include those with family, friends, spouses, work colleagues, and bosses. It is also the reason many of us struggle to be true to ourselves, as we are often fearful of the disapproval we may face as a result.

Role Models

Another interesting way in which we adapt to the world around us is the process of modelling ourselves on others. The term *modelling* refers to the act of copying the behaviours and characteristics of another person.

Each of us, at some stage in our early development, picks a person or several people as role models. A role model can be a family member, celebrity, or even a fictional character.

When we model another person we copy their behaviour, mannerisms, and even aspects of their belief system. Often it is the quality of the role models we choose early on in life that determines the quality of the lives we have in adulthood.

The effects and influence of television and other media on the young has been widely debated, and for good reason. Left unchecked, children will model themselves on any individual who seems to fill an inner need, regardless of the values or beliefs this person may possess.

This can have a tremendous impact on children, as the personality traits, behaviour, and attitudes they imitate may have far-reaching and damaging consequences in later life.

Traumatic Experiences

During much of our early childhood we are incredibly sensitive to our surroundings and deeply affected by the people with whom we interact and develop bonds. As a result of this we can become disturbed and traumatised by a variety of experiences.

These experiences can be child abuse, break-up of the family unit, death of a family member, or some other highly stressful event.

Each of these experiences has the potential to leave mental and emotional scars on us, noticeable only when we are much older. These emotional scars can take the form of low self-esteem and a variety of mental disorders, including depression.

The majority of people who suffer from these conditions spend much of their time suppressing their unresolved issues so they can lead relatively normal lives.

But these suppressed feelings never really go away; they are always present in one form or another, just below the surface.

14

The act of suppressing our uncomfortable thoughts and feelings drains us of energy and begins at some point to affect our general health and wellbeing.

Also, it can cause us to develop a dependency on whatever we use to suppress these feelings, which is the main reason we develop addictions to alcohol, drugs, food, and even TV. In fact, almost every addiction starts out as a method of easing some form of emotional pain.

We live in a world where there are many types of healing therapies available. Most are ineffective, however, because they fail to tackle the root cause of the suffering, namely the damaging beliefs and concepts we have created as result of painful childhood experiences.

The Past Is Over

As you work though this material you will slowly begin to realise that many of your present issues have their roots in your early childhood years.

However, this is not an excuse to start assigning blame to the people responsible for your care during your childhood, as they were simply doing the best they could under the circumstances. Nor is it necessary to start analysing and dissecting what happened in your past.

Ultimately, the only way to resolve childhood issues and traumas is, strangely, not to focus on the past but to recognise the reality of your present life, meet the challenges that appear, and overcome them.

In the next chapter, we will explore the part our minds play in our growth to adulthood.

15

CHAPTER

TWO

The Mind

*Be careful of what you say or think as your mind
is always listening.*

Your Faithful Servant

What is the mind? How does it operate? Is it just another computer? Questions like these have fuelled debates, discussions, and a vast number of scientific studies in attempt to uncover the answers.

This is truly a fascinating subject and one that I would love to explore. However, the purpose of this chapter is not to present an academic study on the mysteries of the human mind, but rather to offer just a short summary on how it operates in our lives.

Let me start by saying that you are really three beings in one, namely:

- The mind (mental, psychological, intellectual)
- The body (physical, biological, organic)
- The spirit (soul, being, higher self)

The mind and body are two vital aspects of your existence, each performing an important function and contributing to your overall life experience. The spirit, on the other hand, is the silent entity within, which patiently observes the actions of the mind and body as you go about your daily life.

Western society puts much of its focus on the mind and the body and neglects the spiritual part of our being. This, in many ways, is the cause of most of the difficulties we experience, as we have become so identified with our minds that we assume this is who we really are.

The mind is that part of you that is the storehouse for all your thoughts, beliefs, and memories. As you grow and develop from childhood the power and influence of your mind grows with you.

Much like a loyal servant, your mind works tirelessly on your behalf. It is not evil, nor does it look to inflict harm or suffering on you. In fact, it cares only about one thing, the fulfilment of every belief and idea impressed upon it.

The Conscious and the Unconscious

The *conscious* and the *unconscious* are names given to the two parts of your mind, which together control virtually every area of your life.

The conscious mind is what you are using to read and understand these words; it is the part of you that evaluates the world around you and then interprets that information in order to make new choices.

The unconscious mind is the silent powerhouse that controls everything in your body. It regulates your heartbeat and digestive system, instructs your cells to continue replenishing themselves, and keeps all your vital organs running in perfect working order.

The unconscious is that part of your mind that contains all your memories and beliefs about life of which you are not consciously aware.

It is the supreme ruler over your physical existence and has an almost infinite capacity to process and store information. It is the source of all your thoughts and emotions, and greatly influences your ability to function in the world.

Think of your unconscious mind as a giant lake, with all the thoughts and memories you have accumulated since the time of your birth floating under the surface.

For the most part, you are totally unaware of the vast amount of information stored within it; that is, until you attempt to recall something or an external event triggers a memory to spontaneously come to the surface into your conscious awareness.

Attached to many of these memories are thoughts and feelings that can affect your behaviour in a variety of ways.

The Thinking Machine

Below the level of your conscious awareness your mind is processing everything it perceives in your environment through your five senses.

Whatever you see, hear, taste, touch, or smell is relayed back to the unconscious part of your mind, which analyses all the information and decides whether or not any of it requires your conscious attention.

The unconscious sorts this information by creating an inner dialogue that sounds something like this:

What's happening right now?

What should I do?

Your unconscious answers the first question by referring to the beliefs it has accumulated up to that point and then based on what it finds it responds to the second question.

For example, imagine you are walking down a darkened street late at night and you hear footsteps behind you. Upon receiving this data, your unconscious mind immediately asks the question "What's happening right now?", and based on the beliefs you have accumulated up to that point, it may conclude that you are in danger.

In answering the second question, "What should I do?" your unconscious may instruct "Run" or "Get away", and as a result you may start to experience feelings of anxiety, together with increases in your breathing, heart rate, and blood flow, all designed to enable you to run as fast as you can.

Your unconscious reacts this way only if your beliefs direct it to do so. If, on the other hand your belief system says you are safe walking down a darkened street at night, you probably won't even notice the footsteps and will simply continue on your way.

Your mind was created for this purpose, to constantly evaluate the world around you based on the beliefs with which it has been programmed; this it does continuously without fail throughout your life.

This constant monitoring of the world around you creates a constant stream of thoughts and is the activity you recognise as thinking.

When I talk about thoughts, I am describing everything that passes through your mind during the course of your life:

- Beliefs
- Ideas
- Opinions

A conservative estimate suggests that there are some fifty thousand thoughts passing through your mind on a daily basis, most of which are negative in nature.

As a result of this constant mental activity, you may forget they are simply thoughts and not reality. Also, you may become so absorbed by them that they distort and confuse your perception about what's truly happening in your daily experience.

When your thoughts become entwined with your emotions you become detached from reality and identify totally with what you are feeling.

You no longer say, "I feel angry," but "I am angry;" or "I feel scared," but "I am scared." It is at this point that you lose touch with who you are and become totally influenced by the intense emotionally charged thoughts flowing through your mind.

Almost like a continual radio drama, you start to believe that the internal dialogue going on inside your head is you, when in reality it is only an aspect of your busy mind.

So If I'm Not My Mind, Who Am I?

Many authors tend to avoid this subject in an attempt to spare the feelings of their readers, but a true explanation of the role your mind plays in your life cannot avoid the topic of spirituality.

You are, in fact, a spiritual being experiencing a temporary physical existence; your mind and body are simply vessels that allow you to function in the world.

As you go through daily life you are not always aware of this aspect of your nature due to the vast number of thoughts absorbing your attention and focus.

Only when the mind becomes quiet and still through prayer or meditation do you begin to get a glimpse of the infinite part of your being, which is beyond the power of words to describe.

This is your spiritual core; it is ageless, wise, and all-powerful. It is the part of you that is always there in the background behind the constant noise of your thoughts, patiently watching as the drama of your life unfolds.

It Wishes Only to Serve

Your mind is not a mysterious entity that needs to be analysed or understood; it is simply a storage area for all your memories, thoughts, and beliefs.

Your mind is not interested in your personal welfare or happiness; it cares only about one thing: to fulfil all the instructions it receives in accordance with the conditioned beliefs created by you. It will continue to do this without fail until the beliefs are either changed or eliminated.

In the next chapter we will explore the incredible influence our beliefs have over our minds and our lives.

CHAPTER
THREE

The Awesome Power of Beliefs

*Our beliefs are the laws we live by regardless of whether they
are true or false.*

Belief Kills and Belief Cures

There is an old West Indian saying, "Belief kills and belief
cures," which means that no matter what you believe to be true
in life, whether it be good or bad, you will reap the harvest of it.

As you have already learned, your mind doesn't differentiate or
judge; it simply accepts as truth whatever you feed it. This is
both a blessing and a curse, as you can become a prisoner of the
beliefs that do not serve you.

All the limiting concepts and ideas you currently hold about
yourself and the world are the root causes of the problems and
difficulties you experience in your life; they affect your
relationships, your health, and even your level of financial
success.

So What Are Beliefs?

Beliefs are simply thoughts linked to emotions that create a
feeling of certainty. This usually manifests as a sensation of
energy in your chest or stomach area.

The feeling originates from an unconscious memory about an
earlier experience, usually one that relates to the time when the
belief was first created.

All your beliefs are formed by a very simple process: you first
experience an **event** in your life, and based on how you
interpret it, you make a **decision** about it. This decision is then

26

stored away in the unconscious and forms the basis of your new **belief**.

The following diagram illustrates this process, which operates continually throughout your life:

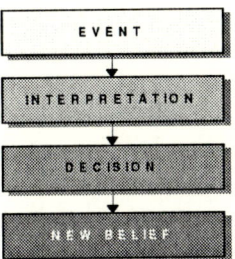

The conclusions stored in your unconscious mind remain there until an event brings them to the surface. It is only when an external event "pushes your buttons" that you become aware of these hidden beliefs. You may be quite surprised or even shocked by how they affect you.

How Do Beliefs Affect Us?

The following diagram illustrates how your beliefs affect almost every single area of your life:

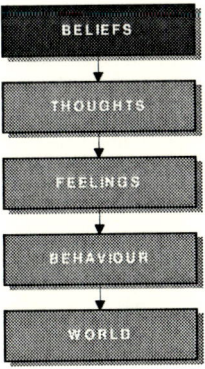

When triggered by an external event, your **beliefs** create a stream of **thoughts**, which then create **feelings** that are designed to motivate you to behave in a certain way. Your **behaviour**, in turn, creates your **world**.

This chain reaction occurs continuously every day of your life, often below your level of conscious awareness.

John's Story

John is a three-year-old boy playing outside his parents' home on a warm summer day; in an instant he wanders out of his mother's sight and sneaks into the next door neighbour's garden.

The neighbour has a large swimming pool and as John walks to the edge of it, someone spots him and screams; this startles John and causes him to trip and fall head first into the deep end of the pool.

The neighbours panic and dive in after him; they manage to get him out quickly and frantically perform mouth-to-mouth resuscitation as he is now unconscious.

Luckily John is revived and walks away from the experience a little shaken but okay. His parents are now very protective of him and always tell him to be careful whenever he is near a pool or the ocean.

Years pass and John is now an adult with a deeply entrenched fear of swimming pools and water. He hardly ever goes to the beach, and despite several attempts he has been unable to learn to swim.

What happened to John is what actually happens to many of us; we experience an event in childhood and then make a judgement based on our interpretation of it.

28

In John's case he made the decision that swimming pools are dangerous, and his judgement expanded to all things related to this activity.

John's experience when he was three years old was actually forgotten by his conscious mind, but his unconscious mind kept an accurate record of the event and the decision he made about it.

This **belief** lay dormant within him until triggered by an event, such as a discussion with a friend, reading a book, or watching TV; whenever such an event occurred, his unconscious mind would quickly remind him of his earlier decision.

Those reminders would first take the form of fear-based **thoughts**, which would trigger **feelings** of anxiety or fear in an attempt to alter his **behaviour.**

Again, this is what the mind is always attempting to do: fulfil its programming in line with our belief systems. From this perspective, the mind is simply doing its job based on the information given to it.

To resolve this issue in his life, John could perhaps see a therapist with whom he could discuss his irrational fear and over a period of time he might uncover the cause of his anxieties and be able to discard the limiting belief.

Irrational fears such as John's, which are based on the limiting beliefs we hold about ourselves and our world, keep the vast majority of us from creating the success we so desperately seek.

The following are true stories that further illustrate the incredible power of beliefs.

Roger Bannister

Roger Bannister is best known as the first human to run a mile in under four minutes. Prior to his successful attempt, it was widely assumed to be impossible for a human being to run a mile within that time frame.

Bannister believed he could, and he used his knowledge as a physician to train and pursue his goal. He did this in 1954 and achieved his dream that year, running the mile in three minutes fifty-nine point four seconds.

His belief defied what everyone else believed, and he was able to break the record and become a legend.

An interesting aspect of this story is the fact that several months later other athletes, some of them college students, started breaking the four-minute mile record just as Bannister had.

It appears that as the psychological barrier was shattered and the world now accepted the **belief** that a human could indeed run a mile in under four minutes, athletes all over the globe began to emulate Bannister's phenomenal achievement.

Going to the Moon

On May 25th, 1961, John F Kennedy, the President of the United States, made a speech in which he stated his **belief** and goal that the US would put a man on the moon by the end of the decade.

The Soviet Union, at the time, was leading the way in the space race, and some thought the goal was just a pipe dream of the youngest president ever elected.

Despite this, the country was inspired by Kennedy's belief in what America could achieve, and many scientists began asking the question "how" rather than "if" it was possible.

The US space program began in the early 1960s with unmanned spacecraft photographing the moon's surface. The program continued to grow while at the same time pushing the frontiers of science and technology until in 1969 it achieved its goal and the first men landed on the moon.

President Kennedy was dead by this time, assassinated in 1963; however, his vision had been achieved.

Kennedy's belief that America could put a man on the moon despite the odds inspired a nation to see the possibility of what could be achieved and in the process gave birth to mankind's quest to explore the stars.

The Amazing Story of Multiple Personality Disorders

Multiple Personality Disorder is an unusual condition in which two or more distinct personalities inhabit a single body. People who suffer from this disorder will regularly change from one personality to another during periods of extreme stress.

These personalities will usually be totally different from each other and exhibit different physical and mental characteristics.

There are incredible documented reports about the mental and physiological changes that occur when individuals who suffer from these disorders switch personalities.

Dr. Bennet Braun of the International Society for the Study of Multiple Personality Disorders in Chicago once documented a case in which all of a patient's subpersonalities except one were allergic to orange juice.

When this particular sufferer drank orange juice while one of his allergic personalities was in control, he would break out in a terrible rash. But as soon as he switched to his nonallergic personality, the rash would instantly start to fade and he could drink orange juice freely.

Allergies are not the only thing that "multiples" can switch on and off. There is also an example that demonstrates the mind's ability to overcome the effects of alcohol: by changing personalities, a multiple who is drunk can instantly become sober. It has even been noted that different personalities existing within the same individual can have alternative reactions to the same drugs.

Other conditions that can vary from personality to personality include scars, cysts, and left- and right-handedness. One personality can even be colour-blind while the others are not, and there have been reports of sufferers changing the colour of their eyes when they switched between identities.

The power of belief in these individuals is so strong that it causes a complete change in their physiology, which continues to baffle scientists.

The Placebo Effect

Another amazing example of the power of belief comes from the story of a terminal cancer patient who was given only a short time to live.

The patient had been struggling with advanced cancer of the lymph nodes, which resulted in the development of tumours all over his body, some of them the size of oranges.

Desperate to find a cure, the patient somehow learned about an experimental cancer drug called Krebiozen. Although his diagnosis was terminal and his chances of survival were virtually non-existent, he begged his physician to give him the drug in a last ditch effort to save himself.

Although a little reluctant, the doctor decided to treat the patient with the new medication. Secretly he did not hold out any hope of the patient surviving even the weekend, as the cancer had at that point ravaged much of the patient's body.

Incredibly, over a relatively short period of time, the doctor reported that the patient's "orange-sized tumours" had totally dissolved, which resulted in a miraculous improvement in his condition.

The speed of the patient's recovery startled everyone, including the doctor treating him. However, not until a medical journal report that indicated that the drug's effects were not as positive as first thought came out months later, did more startling events begin to occur.

The patient, after reading these reports, became quite depressed and suffered a relapse. After being checked back into the hospital, it was found that his tumours had re-appeared and his condition quickly worsened.

It was at this time the doctor tried a little experiment. He told the patient the previous reports about the drug were incorrect and that he, the doctor, had an improved version with which he would treat the patient.

After injecting the patient with nothing but plain water, the astonishing results the patient had previously experienced repeated themselves. The tumours again began to melt away and the man's condition immediately improved.

Unfortunately, this story does not have a happy ending. Two months later another report came out proclaiming Krebiozen totally ineffective in the treatment of cancer. Upon reading this information the patient's faith was completely destroyed and he died two days later.

There are literally thousands of documented cases similar to the above story. However, despite growing evidence that points to a direct link between a person's mental state and their ability to recover from a wide variety of illnesses, the medical world continues to lean heavily towards the use of medication in the treatment of many conditions.

Reflecting Our Reality

If you have ever wondered what kinds of beliefs you have stored away in your unconscious that silently influence your choices, take a good look at your life, including your friends, your loved ones, your job, and even your health.

The life you currently live is a reflection of your beliefs about what you are willing to accept and tolerate. This is the vital difference that separates people who live abundant happy lives from those who don't.

For instance, people who continue to stay in abusive relationships, work at jobs they don't enjoy, or struggle financially, do so as a result of the beliefs they hold.

Yet there are individuals in society who will never ever accept being unjustly treated, living just above the poverty line, or working in professions that do not make full use of their gifts.

These individuals are those who stand out in the crowd: the entrepreneurs, pioneers, and leaders who refuse to allow the opinions of others to dictate how they live their lives.

They do this not because they are better or more gifted than everyone else, but simply because their beliefs do not allow them to do otherwise.

The Rulebook

It is important to remember that we all play an active role in the creation of our belief systems, even if this occurs when we are vulnerable to the influence of others.

Once these beliefs are impressed on our unconscious mind, they become the rulebook that controls the direction of our lives.

All your successes and failures, then, are in some way influenced by this unconscious set of rules you have written. Whatever it is you wish to achieve, whether it be a skill you're attempting to master, a subject you wish to learn or an illness you are struggling to overcome, your success will be determined by a single factor: the unconscious beliefs that make up your book of rules.

Much of the struggle you experience in life relates to the inner turmoil you feel when you make a new choice that conflicts with the set of rules you have created about life and simply forgotten.

To end this struggle and become the master of your own destiny, you must therefore master the unconscious beliefs that control you.

Another interesting aspect of belief systems is the way in which they operate to create something called comfort zones, which we will explore in the next chapter.

CHAPTER

FOUR

Our Own Personal Prisons

The difference between a comfort zone and a prison cell is that one of them has bars you can see.

Our Zones of Comfort

Many of us, whether we know it or not, live within a prison of our own making. This prison has no metal bars, nor can its walls be seen by the naked eye; however, it is every bit as effective in keeping us from our freedom as a real prison cell. It's called our *comfort zone*.

Most people are not aware they even have comfort zones because they have been happily (or unhappily) living within them for many years.

Often it is only when significant changes occur in their lives or they are forced to adopt a new activity or behaviour that they realise they've been living within a zone of comfort and security.

Examples of these changes:

- Leaving a longstanding relationship
- Starting a new relationship
- Changing careers
- Coming into large sums of money
- Starting and running a business
- Learning a new skill
- Moving to a new neighbourhood or country
- Meeting new people
- Becoming famous
- Achieving the success they've always dreamed of

All of the above have a common theme: they involve a change) of some kind or doing something new and unfamiliar. Most human beings do not like change for this very reason and many try to avoid it at all costs.

How Do Comfort Zones Operate?

A comfort zone is basically an emotional barrier set up by your mind that is meant to keep you safe from harm. It is held in place by your belief system and can be incredibly powerful in controlling your behaviour.

Whenever you attempt to move through your comfort zone you might find it an emotionally painful time during which you experience intense self-doubt, fear, and uncertainty.

Let's say you decide to change your job after working in the same career for twenty years. At first there may not be any initial fear or uncertainty stirred up as a result of this decision; however, as soon as you start to do something that moves you closer to your goal you may begin to feel anxiety and doubt about whether you are making the right decision.

These thoughts and feelings will persist until you either remove the underlying beliefs motivating them or prove to yourself they arc groundless.

We have all experienced this cycle at some time in our lives, whether it was attending the first day of school, moving away to college, starting a new job, leaving home, or getting married.

Some of us are able to make these transitions easily while others can become stuck in a particular comfort zone and stay there for many years, or even a lifetime.

39

Comfort Zones Come In Different Forms

Comfort zones can take on a variety of different forms, from the area in which you live and the circle of people with whom you socialise, to the amount of money you earn.

The primary force that keeps you living within your zone is your fear-based belief about what will happen if you move outside it.

Regardless of how ridiculous or unrealistic that belief may be, you will accept it as truth depending on the level of certainty you feel.

Your comfort zone is not really comfortable at all, but is really a virtual prison that keeps you from evolving and growing as a human being.

The bars to that prison are your fears about what may possibly happen if you move beyond them. The key to your freedom therefore lies in the removal of the underlying beliefs that cause those fears to exist.

What's Outside Your Zone?

Just for a moment think about a goal or dream you have that seems somehow out of reach. Now check to see if achieving it requires that you move out of your comfort zone and into unfamiliar territory.

It could be a dream job, a new relationship, starting your own business, losing weight, or living in a totally different part of the world.

As you do this little exercise notice how a subtle feeling of fear or nervousness begins to emerge in your chest or stomach area.

This is your unconscious mind springing into action with the intention of dissuading you from doing anything it perceives may put you in danger.

Most of the time you won't notice the constant influence your comfort zone plays in your life, and you might find yourself placing the blame for your lack of progress towards your goals on laziness or procrastination.

However, if you stop and consider just for a moment why you can't seem to get that item crossed off your to-do list, make that phone call, or fill out that application, you will begin to realise the true cause: **What you want to do is outside your comfort zone.**

Again, it is your beliefs that direct your mind to do this; therefore, in order to break through your self-imposed limitations and achieve the success you desire, you will need to remove them.

In the next chapter you will learn a powerful process that will allow you to do just that, and do so in the fastest way possible.

CHAPTER

FIVE

The Conscious Enquiry Technique™

The key to transformation comes from asking the right questions and allowing the answers to unfold.

The Power of Asking

Ask, and it will be given to you; search, and you will find; knock, and the door will be opened for you. For everyone who asks receives, and everyone who searches finds, and for everyone who knocks, the door will be opened.

Matthew 7:7-8

The above passage from the Gospel of Matthew provided me with vital clues to creating the powerful tools you are about to learn.

It was after reading this passage as part of my research that I made an awesome discovery.

I found that by using the power of specific questions, I could direct my mind to achieve any result I desired and do so within seconds.

Since that time I have refined the process and developed a technique of immense power that has allowed me to create rapid changes not only in my own life, but also in the lives of the clients I coach.

I call it **The Conscious Enquiry Technique™** or CE because that in essence is what it is. It's a technique that allows you to consciously call upon hidden abilities and states within you.

The technique is very simple and takes only a few minutes to learn, but once you have, you can start to apply it immediately in a variety of ways, such as:

- Accessing resourceful states
- Healing emotional wounds
- Programming your mind to achieve any goal
- Permanently erasing limiting beliefs
- Improving relationships

This is not a complete list, as I am currently developing even more applications of this powerful tool, some of which will be included in the revised edition of this manual.

Key Principles

There are some key principles that form the backbone of this technique:

- You are not your mind
- Your mind will answer any question you ask
- Any ability or skill you have ever demonstrated is a resource you can call upon

You are not your mind

Your mind is the sum total of all your experiences. It is your faithful servant and will do its utmost to serve you in accordance with your belief system. It is in essence a bio-computer designed to help you adapt and survive in the world.

Your mind will answer any question you ask

Have you ever asked yourself the question, "Why am I so stupid?" I bet the answer you got wasn't a very nice one. The reason for this is that your mind looks at every question you ask as a request for information and it will do everything in its power to respond to it.

Unfortunately, we can be led into trouble by the quality of some of the questions we ask ourselves:

- Why am I so crappy at this job?
- Why can't I ever make it?
- Why does everyone dump on me?
- Why is life so unfair?

Can you imagine the types of answers that come back to you when you habitually ask these types of questions?

Now let's look at another set of questions.

- What can I do to make a success of this job?
- What do I need to do in order to overcome this obstacle?
- What do I need to do in order to achieve this goal?
- How can I solve this problem?

Given this set of questions you automatically tap into resources that give you solutions to the problems you are facing, as opposed to the previous examples, which merely reinforce them.

This is exactly what your mind was designed to do: answer questions based on past information and relay the answers back to you.

Any ability or skill you have ever demonstrated is a resource you can call upon

When I started studying various forms of accelerated learning many years ago, I was amazed to discover that every experience we have ever had from the time we were born is stored in minute detail in our unconscious minds, and that our problem is not storing the information, but rather recalling it at a later date.

Studies have shown that individuals regressed through the use of hypnosis find they can recall the sights, sounds, smells, and tastes locked within memories decades old.

Professor Wilder Penfield, a Canadian surgeon, made an interesting discovery while performing a medical procedure on several of his epilepsy patients; it involved examining the brain tissue of his patients while they were under a local anaesthetic.

He was amazed to find that when he touched certain individual cells, his patients would suddenly recall experiences from their pasts.

The patients would later say they didn't just recall the experience but relived it as if they were actually there, complete with tastes, smells, noises, colours, and feelings. The clarity of the memories was the same regardless of whether they were a few hours or many years old.

Professor Penfield suggests that within each cell of the brain is the perfect memory of every event in our lives, and if we can find the right stimulus we can experience each one all over again.

How Does Conscious Enquiry Work?

The Conscious Enquiry Technique™ works when you simply ask a question and become still while the answer arises in your conscious mind. The answer can result in access to beneficial states, such as inner peace and happiness, or dormant skills and abilities.

In this chapter we will be using the Conscious Enquiry Technique™ to gain access to the natural ability we all have to erase limiting beliefs.

Ground Rules

Before we begin there are some ground rules that require your attention.

- Please abstain from alcohol and any mind-altering substances during these exercises, as this may interfere with the experience.

- Please ensure there are no distractions in your immediate environment, such as TVs or loud music, as this process requires several minutes of focused attention.

- Please do not use this technique while driving or operating any machinery that requires any level of concentration.

Erasing limiting beliefs by using The Conscious Enquiry Technique™ is a simple process, detailed as follows.

How to Erase a Belief

Step 1: Identify the limiting belief

Whenever you decide to remove a limiting belief it is vitally important that you are clear on what the belief actually is. You can do this either by writing it down or repeating it to yourself verbally. Also, please ensure that you only work on **one** belief at a time.

Examples:

- I'm overworked
- I don't understand my computer
- I get nervous when I talk to people of the opposite sex
- I don't know what I want
- I'm too old
- I'm too young
- I'm stuck in my career

Step 2: Apply the Conscious Enquiry Technique™

A. Experience the Belief

What you will be doing in this step is to **experience the energy behind the belief.** All beliefs have a certain amount of energy; this comes from the experiences that are stored in our unconscious mind. These buried memories provide the "evidence" that our belief is true.

The energy I am referring to will be the underlying emotions, such as fear, anger, or grief that the belief stirs up within us.

The energy behind each belief will vary in intensity depending on the level of certainty we feel; this is due to the level of emotion that was present at the time the belief was created, together with the number of times it was reinforced.

It is not important to analyse or identify an emotion that is associated with a belief at this or any other stage of this process, as it is just energy that has manifested as a result of a belief and our primary focus here is simply to erase it.

To experience this energy all you have to do is **notice where it manifests in your body.** This will usually be in your chest or stomach area. Once you have identified where the energy is simply allow yourself to **feel** it **for five seconds.**

B. Erase the belief

In this part of the process you will use the following question to direct your mind to erase the energy behind the belief:

"Where is that ability within me to erase this energy?"

It is very important that you ask this question with the intention of getting an answer, even if you do not know what the answer will be.

For example, imagine that something of value had been mislaid in your home, such as your keys. If you were to ask the question, "Where are my keys?" you would do so with a genuine belief that the keys were somewhere in your home and with a sense of curiosity about where they were.

When you ask the Conscious Enquiry question do so in the same spirit, just as you would if you had lost your keys and wanted to find them.

Once you have asked the CE question, simply be **curious** about where that ability is and wait for a minimum of **ten seconds**. To help keep your mind focused, mentally count from one to ten.

The reason we allow a ten second pause is because this is roughly the length of time the unconscious needs to seek out an answer. After you ask a CE question you will experience a subtle shift in how you feel as some of the emotional energy starts to disappear.

This experience varies for each person; some feel a sense of lightness, relaxation, and even a calming of their thoughts as their minds become quieter, while others just sense the movement of energy through their bodies.

Regardless of the experience you have, simply go back to step two and repeat the process as illustrated in the following diagram.

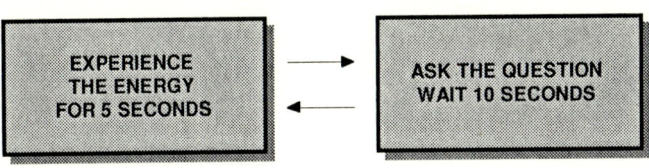

By repeating the process of experiencing the energy and asking the questions, you are gradually erasing all the unconscious thoughts and memories that create the feeling of certainty behind a belief.

By the time you ask the question on the fourth or fifth round, the energy should be completely erased. Without this energy you no longer have a belief but merely a thought, which has no meaning to you.

After completing the steps outlined above, take a fresh look at the belief you were working on and ask yourself: **Do I still believe this?**

If you have completely erased all the energy behind the belief you may surprise yourself as you answer with a simple, "No".

This may feel a little strange at first, but after several minutes you should feel a profound sense freedom and peace as you begin to realise that the belief is no longer a part of you.

This entire process usually takes about **three minutes** to complete regardless of how long you have had the belief.

Unblocking Procedure

If you find that after going through the process five times there is still some energy remaining, you may have encountered an unconscious belief that is blocking you. This is something that occurs from time to time when you start to apply the Conscious Enquiry Technique™ on a regular basis.

51

These beliefs can range from doubts about the effectiveness of the process or even worse and much more subtle, fear relating to what may happen if you actually succeed and achieve the results you desire.

Regardless of the underlying reasons for the block there is a simple solution, which can be applied whenever you experience this problem. This involves using The Conscious Enquiry Technique™ to eliminate the unconscious conflict preventing you from making progress.

How to Erase a Block

Step 1: Acknowledge the block

Whenever you experience any difficulty with this or any other technique in this manual, simply take a step back and **acknowledge** that something is not working; once you have done this you are ready to go to the next step.

Step 2: Apply the Conscious Enquiry Technique™

A. Experience the block

In this step, identify the specific area in your body where the block is located. This will be similar to the energy behind a belief and it will be in either your chest or stomach area.

Although you may not be consciously aware of the reason for the block, it will always manifest itself as energy in one of these two areas and sometimes even in both. It may also be tied to feelings of tension together with thoughts such as "**I can't do this**" or "**It's not working.**"

Fully experience the energy you have identified as the block and allow yourself to simply be with it for about five seconds.

B. Erase the block

To erase this energy use the following CE question, which in this example is the same as the one we employ when erasing beliefs:

"Where is that ability within me to erase that energy?"

After asking this question be curious and wait for ten seconds as your mind seeks out the ability within you. Once the ten seconds have elapsed you will again experience a shift in energy, which will result in a reduction in the resistance you experience.

After this has occurred simply repeat steps A and B until the energy behind the block is **completely** erased, and return to the original process you were working on.

But Will It Work for Me?

This technique will work for anyone who applies it for this very simple reason: You have been changing and modifying your beliefs throughout your life; if this were not the case you never would have been able to mature from a child into the person you are now.

What you've done in the past, however, is to look for evidence in the outside world before you changed or discarded a belief; what you are now learning is how to gain access to this ability at will.

Practice Session

In this practice session we are going to work on erasing a single belief that is stopping you from moving forward in a particular area of your life. For those of you who are reading this material and experiencing disbelief that this is even possible, I suggest you work on the belief, **"This will not work for me."**

The reason I highlighted this belief is that it may prevent you from fully experiencing the tremendous power of this process. This is the nature of beliefs; they will always attempt to prove themselves right regardless of what you consciously desire.

However, if you are feeling optimistic about this process, then feel free to focus on another belief.

Examples:

* I'm so disorganised
* I'm going to fail
* I can't change
* I'll never get over this
* I don't know what to do
* I'm never going to achieve....

Once you have identified such a belief simply follow the instructions detailed below. As this will be your first experience working with this process, allow yourself ten minutes for this exercise.

Erase a Belief

Step 1: Identify the limiting belief

I believe:_____

Step 2: Apply the Conscious Enquiry Technique™

A.   Experience the Belief

Experience the energy behind this belief for **five seconds**.

(You will feel the energy in either your chest or stomach area.)

B.   Erase the belief

Ask the following Conscious Enquiry Question:

"Where is that ability within me to erase that energy?"

Pause and wait **ten seconds**.

Repeat steps A and B until the belief is erased.

Note: If there is still any energy remaining after repeating steps A and B five times, stop and use the **unblocking procedure,** then start again.

Unblocking Procedure

Step 1: Acknowledge the block

If you experience any difficulty with a particular process, allow yourself to step back and acknowledge that something isn't working.

Step 2: Apply the Conscious Enquiry Technique™

A. Experience the block

Experience the energy behind the block for **five seconds**.

(You will feel the energy in either your chest or stomach area.)

B. Erase the block

Ask the following Conscious Enquiry Question:

"Where is that ability within me to erase that energy?"

Pause and wait **ten seconds**.

Repeat steps A and B until the block is completely erased.

What You May Experience

After completing the above process you will find that the belief you once had no longer stirs up any feelings within you, and as a result your attitude and perceptions will undergo a significant change.

You may also find that without even trying you feel more positive and confident, and it may even feel as if you never had the old limiting belief at all.

How Can This Technique Help You?

Taking into consideration everything you now understand about the incredible power of beliefs, what would the ability to erase any belief in under three minutes allow you to create in your life?

The answer is…anything you desire!

This single application of the Conscious Enquiry Technique™ can help you achieve truly amazing results. Whether it's a skill you wish to master, a problem you're trying to solve, or a goal you wish to achieve, the possibilities are endless.

By erasing the limiting beliefs you have about yourself and your world you are freeing yourself from the prison of your past conditioning and allowing the hidden resources within you to come forth.

In the next couple of chapters we will further explore how we can apply this powerful tool to a variety of areas, starting with how to become virtually problem-free.

CHAPTER

SIX

Become Problem-Free

Do not struggle with problems; simply look beyond them and recognise the truth.

Many Problems, One Solution

In this chapter we explore the root cause of all problems and obstacles and learn how to easily overcome them by applying the Conscious Enquiry Technique™.

After completing this chapter you will know and understand the true nature of all problems and be able to create solutions quickly and easily.

The Truth About Problems

The simple truth about problems is that they are just another set of beliefs we've created about our world. For example:

- I don't have enough money
- I'm not smart enough
- I can't find a job I enjoy
- I don't know how to improve my marriage

What we actually perceive as problems are simply situations or events that need to be either accepted or dealt with. To prove this point, think for a moment about all the problems in the world such as global warming, political unrest, wars, hunger, and the spread of disease.

Now, just for a second, imagine a world with no people in it, not one single soul. All that's left are empty cities and buildings and wildlife roaming free.

After picturing this image in your mind for a few seconds, try to locate all the problems you thought of a moment ago.

What you will find is that without people in the picture **there are no problems**; there is nothing to discuss, change, complain about, or fix; the world is simply as it is.

This is due to the simple truth that the term 'problem' is simply a label we attach to particular events or situations in our lives, and as such are totally dependent on the beliefs we hold about them.

Whenever you attempt to solve any problem, what you are really doing is struggling to see past your own limited way of thinking. The solution you are trying to find already exists; you are simply unable to see it.

Again, this is because your mind takes everything you say or think literally. So when you believe you have a "huge problem", the mind hears this and goes to work to make that belief a reality.

If any of this seems a little confusing it is only because you have the belief that your problems are real and difficult to solve. However, this view is just another set of concepts and ideas created by you as a result of your past conditioning.

Whenever you look at the world around you, you see not always through your eyes but rather through the frame of what your beliefs allow you to see.

To give you an example of this, think of a time when you looked for something in your home you thought you had mislaid.

You looked up and down, in every conceivable place you could think of and still you couldn't find it. Eventually, after you had finally given up, you realised the very thing you were searching for was right in front of you the whole time.

What happened to you is something that happens to all of us at some time. Because you were convinced you had lost something, your mind took the information literally and as a result made the very object you were looking for invisible to you.

It was only when you gave up the search in frustration - and thus stopped the flow of limiting thoughts - that you truly began to see clearly again.

When you react to an event in your life and make the decision it's a problem, you send a powerful message to your mind. It, in turn, does its best to ensure that what you believe becomes a reality and will, in effect, block you from seeing even the simplest solution.

The Difference

Problems and obstacles are very similar: they are both labels we attach to events that occur in our lives, and they both challenge and test us to our limits.

However, there is a subtle difference between them. Problems are issues that prevent us from achieving some hidden objective that we are not aware of.

Obstacles, on the other hand, are very similar to problems, except that we are fully aware of what they are preventing us from moving towards.

The difference between problems and obstacles, then, comes from the level of awareness we have about an issue in our lives at any given time.

This is the true nature of all problems: they are simply obstacles to some hidden objective we are simply not aware of, and are ultimately just another set of limiting beliefs we hold about our world.

The Path

Your life is very much like a journey along a winding path that has many detours, hills, and valleys. For some, the journey is long and difficult; for others it can seem very fast with only the occasional bump; for a special few, it is a blissful journey of discovery.

For most people, life is very much like the first example and seems a tough and demanding experience. This has much to do with the baggage people carry in the form of limiting beliefs and it is this extra burden that makes the journey so difficult.

This is exactly how I see my own life: as a long journey during which I occasionally experience obstacles and dilemmas that appear to block me from getting to my destination.

As a result of this philosophy I no longer seek answers in the external world, as I know they already reside within me.

I accept full responsibility for the challenges and difficulties I face in my life, and I see them in some way as creations of my mind, born either of the poor choices I have made in the past or my present attitude towards them.

Therefore, since my mind created my problems, I use the same mind to find the solutions, which it easily does once I realise the simple truth: **a problem is just another belief**.

By allowing yourself to start looking at the problems and issues in your life from this new perspective, you will find that your attitude to them will shift considerably.

61

How to Erase Any Problem or Obstacle

The procedure for solving problems and overcoming obstacles is a simple two step process, which is detailed below:

Step 1: Identify

Whenever you are faced with any obstacle or problem, no matter how huge or overwhelming, the most important thing you can do is to identify what the problem actually is; do this either by writing it down or repeating it out loud to yourself.

Once you have clearly identified the problem, you are ready to go to the next step.

Step 2: Apply the Conscious Enquiry Technique™

Erase the belief you have identified. Do this until you have absolutely no sense of any energy behind the belief and can categorically state that you no longer believe it to be true.

Once you have arrived at this point you may decide that there is nothing further you need to do as the problem may simply have become a situation that requires your attention.

By erasing the belief that a problem exists you will become aware of amazingly simple solutions. This is a powerful way to apply the Conscious Enquiry Technique™, as it allows you to easily create solutions to the problems and difficulties you experience in daily life.

Practice Session

What I would now like you to do is think about a particular problem or obstacle in your life that is presently causing you difficulty.

Examples:

- I can't communicate with my spouse
- I don't know what to do
- I have no idea what my ideal career is
- I have huge debts
- My sales figures are down
- I can't figure this out

Once you have identified such a problem simply follow the steps below.

Erase a Problem/Obstacle

Step 1: Identify the problem or obstacle

My problem/obstacle is:_____

Step 2: Apply the Conscious Enquiry Technique™

A.   Experience the belief

Experience the energy behind your belief for **five seconds.**

(You will feel the energy in either your chest or stomach area.)

B.   Erase the belief

Ask the following Conscious Enquiry Question:

"Where is that ability within me to erase that energy?"

Pause and wait **ten seconds.**

Repeat steps A and B until the belief is erased.

Note: If there is still any energy remaining after repeating steps A and B five times, stop and use the **unblocking procedure** and start again.

Unblocking Procedure

Step 1: Acknowledge the block

If you experience any difficulty with a particular process, allow yourself to step back and acknowledge that something isn't working.

Step 2: Apply the Conscious Enquiry Technique™

A. Experience the block

Experience the energy behind the block for **five seconds**.

(You will feel the energy in either your chest or stomach area.)

B. Erase the block

Ask the following Conscious Enquiry Question:

"Where is that ability within me to erase that energy?"

Pause and wait **ten seconds**.

Repeat steps A and B until the block is completely erased.

As I stated earlier, you may now feel there is nothing you need to do, or alternatively you may get sudden radical new ideas and solutions to problems that previously seemed unsolvable.

Whatever you experience, simply allow your intuition to guide you to take the most appropriate action.

Solve Any Problem?

What you have learned in this chapter may challenge some of your conventional ideas about the nature of problems and how to solve them. This is as it should be.

The true reality of life is that all problems are really just labels (beliefs) we have attached to events or situations in our lives. Therefore, in order to solve them, all we need to do is remove the label and move towards the solution.

It makes no difference whether the problem refers to how to heal your relationship, bring your business back to profitability, or discover your ideal career. All problems are essentially creations of your mind and it is by using the mind to undo what it has created that we find the answers.

The technique works equally well in the area of scientific research, business development and strategy, and even when applied to social and economic problems.

There really is no limit to the wide variety of problems that can be solved using this simple process.

Experience it for yourself!

In the next chapter we will discover how to overcome one of the biggest obstacles to a happy and abundant life - fear!

CHAPTER

SEVEN

The Illusion of Fear

Fear comes from the illusion that you cannot handle what the future holds.

The Enemy Within

In this chapter we are going to tackle one of the biggest causes of pain and suffering in the known world - fear.

Fear is a major reason many of us fail to have the fulfilling and rewarding life we all so desperately seek. It is also without doubt the number one factor holding back the human race.

Fear is the root cause of greed, hate, envy, anger, and every other negative emotion you can imagine. In fact, if I were able to wave a magic wand at this very moment and remove this emotion from every human being on the planet, our world would be totally transformed.

Greed, for instance, comes from the fear that there isn't enough to go around, which creates an insatiable hunger within us to take as much as we can from others.

Envy relates to how we feel about the achievements, possessions, and gifts others have and stems from the fear that we will never have those things for ourselves.

Hate originates from the fear that somehow we will be harmed by others. Whenever we truly hate or dislike someone, we are experiencing the fear of what we believe that person will do to us.

The Mother of Stress

Stress, the number one killer in the twenty-first century, is nothing more than fear in disguise. In the world of physics stress is defined as:

A force or a system of forces producing deformation and strain.

This is exactly what is happening to many millions of people around the globe right at this very moment. In essence we are continually being pulled in two different directions at the same time and struggling to cope with this impossible situation out of **fear** of what may happen if we don't.

What eventually happens is that we are literally pulled apart, and our minds, as well as our bodies, shut down as a result.

This shutting down can take the form of a physical as well as an emotional breakdown, which can result in the body's immune system cracking under the strain and lead to the development of a variety of illnesses.

Many of us attempt to cope with stress by applying various stress management techniques. However, these yield only short term results because the true cause of our suffering has not been tackled - namely, our fears.

The True Definition of Fear

In order to effectively prevent this emotion from controlling our lives it is important that we fully understand what fear is.

Based on my own personal observations, I have arrived at the following definition:

Fear is a belief relating to some future event that we feel we will be unable to cope with.

This is all that fear is: simply a belief about what may or may not happen in the future. It cannot exist in the past or even in the present moment; it can only affect us as a belief about something yet to happen.

The level of certainty we feel in relation to the belief will determine the level of the fear that is experienced.

At this very moment there are literally billions of people around the world quietly struggling with a wide range of fears and anxieties such as:

- Growing older
- Making decisions
- Being humiliated
- Financial ruin
- Dying
- Illness
- Ending a relationship
- Losing a loved one
- Confrontations
- Public speaking

The list, as you can guess, is endless, yet all the events on the list will occur at some point in the future and are all essentially beliefs that create a strong feeling of certainty within us.

The Key to Self-Confidence

Whenever a client tells me they lack self-confidence, I always ask a simple question:

What are you afraid of?

Some react defensively to this question and say that their lack of confidence has nothing to do with fear but is simply something they need to work on.

This common response highlights an attitude that is quite widespread.

One of the biggest challenges people have is actually facing up to and acknowledging their fears. Many prefer not to talk about the deep seated anxieties that plague their daily lives; instead they prefer to label themselves as individuals with low self-confidence.

Bookstores all over the world are littered with new titles claiming to be able to make us more self-assured and assertive; however, many of these books provide only short-term solutions, while others are totally ineffective.

The reason for this is that self-confidence is just a feeling or state we experience when fear is not present.

Many authors and therapists overlook this simple truth and as a result waste precious time focusing on ill-conceived methods and strategies that do nothing to tackle the true cause of people's problems.

If you truly wish to become a more confident and assertive person you need to acknowledge and confront the fears that control you.

Once you have done this, you are free to use a variety of strategies, such as the one that follows, to eliminate them.

How to Erase Any Fear from Your Life

Step 1: Identify the fear

Clearly identify your fear by breaking it down to a belief that relates to the possible future that is causing you anxiety and worry.

Step 2: Apply the Conscious Enquiry Technique™

When you have clearly identified the belief behind your fear you are ready to use the Conscious Enquiry Technique™ to eliminate it from your mind. By erasing this belief from your consciousness, you will begin to see it as just another thought that has no meaning to you.

Although the experience of working on your fears may be a little uncomfortable to begin with, it will be well worth it once you discover what it feels like to finally be free of the suffering they have caused throughout your life.

Practice Session

What I would like you to do now is to think of a fear that is presently stopping you from moving forward with your life in some way. It does not have to be a huge fear; however, it should be something that is challenging.

Examples:

- If I stand up to my boss, I will get fired
- When I get old no one will want me
- If I make the wrong decision I will be ruined
- If I let a spider rest on my hand it will hurt me
- If I make that speech I will be humiliated

Once you have identified a fear, break it down to a belief about something that is going to occur in the future and then apply the Conscious Enquiry Technique™ as detailed below:

Erase a Fear

Step 1: Identify the limiting belief

I Believe:_____

Step 2: Apply the Conscious Enquiry Technique™

A. Experience the belief

Experience the energy behind this belief for **five seconds.**

(You will feel the energy in either your chest or stomach area.)

B. Erase the belief

Ask the following Conscious Enquiry Question:

"Where is that ability within me to erase that energy?"

Pause and wait **ten seconds.**

Repeat steps A and B until the belief is erased.

Note: If there is still any energy remaining after repeating steps A and B five times, stop and use the **unblocking procedure** and start again.

Unblocking Procedure

Step 1: Acknowledge the block

If you experience any difficulty with a particular process, allow yourself to step back and acknowledge that something isn't working.

Step 2: Apply the Conscious Enquiry Technique™

A. Experience the block

Experience the energy behind the block for **five seconds**.

(You will feel the energy in either your chest or stomach area.)

B. Erase the block

Ask the following Conscious Enquiry Question:

"Where is that ability within me to erase that energy?"

Pause and wait **ten seconds**.

Repeat steps A and B until the block is completely erased.

After completing this exercise you may feel a little strange as you notice that the belief no longer generates an emotional charge within you. This will pass after a few minutes as you become aware of the calm that follows.

A Fearful World

This section is very relevant, if you consider the current world climate of ongoing threats of terrorism, economic uncertainty, and continuing ecological disasters, to name just three.

It may seem at times we live in an anxiety filled world; however, the truth is that the outer world is just a reflection of the fear that exists within and the deep unease many of us feel.

Your fears are often signals from your unconscious that indicate you are about to move through a comfort zone. It is at this critical point that you either rise to the challenge and face your fears or retreat to what you perceive as safe and allow them to control you.

Now that you have an effective method for removing any fear from your life, feel free to use this process on any other fears you may have and eliminate them once and for all.

In the next chapter I will show you how to use a variation of the Conscious Enquiry Technique™ that will allow you achieve any goal you desire.

CHAPTER

EIGHT

The Art of Creation

We are all artists, for in every moment we are creating the masterpiece that is our life.

All Success Is an Act of Creation

In this chapter, I am going to share with you an incredibly powerful process that will allow you to reach any goal you set for yourself and do so at a speed that will amaze you.

There are many people who would have you believe that success and achievement can be accomplished only through hard work and intense discipline coupled with determination and sacrifice.

This, we are told, is why so few step up to the plate and go for their dreams; as most people are not willing to pay the price to reap the rewards of abundant wealth and happiness.

In my view this is far from the truth. I believe the single most important factor that determines success of any kind is having the **conscious** and **unconscious** minds in total **agreement** with each other.

If there is a goal you have been trying to achieve for some time and despite all your efforts you've been unable to make any real progress, it is most likely due to the fact that you are out of sync with the unconscious part of your mind.

Whenever you set goals for yourself not in line with your rulebook or that force you outside your comfort zone, the unconscious mind will do its best to sabotage your efforts by creating barriers to your success.

This sabotage can manifest as fear-based thoughts, feelings, and behaviours that may prevent you from making any progress towards your objectives.

All this stems from the fact that your unconscious mind does not agree with your conscious decision to pursue a particular goal. It does this simply because of the beliefs you have created and stored within it.

This is why it is vitally important to have the full agreement of your unconscious mind when attempting to achieve any goal or objective; failure to do this will result in a continual inner struggle that may delay or permanently block you from its attainment.

To achieve agreement between your conscious and unconscious minds it will be necessary for you to erase all the limiting beliefs you have stored in your unconscious mind that may oppose the goal you wish to achieve. Once this has been completed you will be totally free to create the result you desire.

The process outlined in this chapter will allow you to accomplish this in less than **ten minutes**.

When your unconscious and conscious minds are in total agreement, the achievement of your goal becomes effortless. You may still have to take specific steps to make it a reality, but you will find the journey towards it will be a much smoother one.

Our True Purpose

Many scholars and philosophers have long argued about the true purpose of life, and have all arrived at different answers.

Based on my own studies of a variety of personal growth and spiritual texts over many years, I have come to a simple conclusion:

We are all here to create and to experience the results of those creations.

Regardless of your particular religious or philosophical background, if you carefully think about the above statement you will realise this is what we all actually do.

In every moment we are in the process of creating; we do this through the choices we make about who and what we are from one moment to the next. Each of our choices leads us along a different path, which in turn creates the results we experience.

We are all choice makers, constantly creating new results in our lives. However, most people are totally unaware of this fact, which leads many to live under the illusion that success and achievement are somehow dependent on external forces, or even worse: luck!

Personal Responsibility

An interesting characteristic I have noticed in my studies of exceptionally successful individuals is the way in which they accept total responsibility for their lives.

Regardless of the many failures and hardships they may have endured, they always find a way to bounce back and achieve the impossible.

Taking responsibility is not to be confused with assigning blame, as the two are very different concepts. When you take responsibility you are saying, **"What happens in my life is up to me,"** but when you blame you are condemning others or even yourself for your misfortune.

The act of blaming is both damaging and ultimately a waste of time. Whenever you give away your power in this way you condition yourself for failure.

However, when you take absolute responsibility for your life you send a powerful message to your unconscious that says you are in control of your destiny. Once your mind fully accepts this belief, you will become far more resourceful and self-reliant than you have ever been.

The Obstacles to Creating What We Desire

Many people find the idea of setting goals a painful and confusing one. There are a variety of reasons for this, some of which are detailed as follows:

- **We set the wrong goals**

One of the biggest errors many people make in setting goals in their lives is that they invariably set goals they do not really wish to achieve.

This can be due to the pressures in their life situations or simply that they have lost track of their true purpose. It can also be due to the fact they are simply too afraid to go for what they truly desire.

An easy way to uncover what *you* truly want is simply to ask yourself, **"What makes me happy?"** or **"What would I do if I had absolutely no fear?"**

Questions like these focus your mind on answers that can help you make the right choices.

- **We set too many goals**

There are many self-help authors and gurus who promote the idea of setting anywhere between five and twelve goals at any one time.

The thinking behind this strategy is that setting a goal in each of the different areas of your life, such as family, friends, personal relationships, hobbies, community, and career, will lead to a happier more fulfilling life.

However, the vast majority of people who apply this strategy end up overwhelmed and confused by the increasing number of items they now have on their to-do lists.

What this inevitably leads to is more stress and a feeling of failure when they fail to live up to these unrealistic standards.

Many people avoid setting goals for this very purpose; they start out with the best of intentions but somewhere along the way they lose focus and give up.

To avoid this common pitfall, I suggest you set a maximum of three goals at a time. It is far easier to maintain your focus on three goals throughout your day than five or twelve.

- **We don't believe we can achieve our goals**

A serious block to creating the results you want is the belief that you will never really achieve them. This usually happens, again, at an unconscious level and often results in feelings of apathy causing us to procrastinate rather than take action.

There are exceptions to this rule, but these are usually individuals who struggle and fight their way to their goals in spite of themselves and in many instances they are unable to sustain their success once they achieve it.

If you are currently working on a goal and have found it difficult to achieve, I ask you to look within and ask yourself, **"Do I truly believe I can achieve this?"**

Whatever arises from the depths of your mind is the source of your difficulties and it is this that requires change, rather than what you perceive in the outside world.

How to Set Goals You Will Achieve

The method I am about to show you may contradict what you have previously been taught about goal setting and may even seem over-simplified. However, be warned: this process is extremely powerful.

I have taken everything I have learned over the past twenty years and reduced it to a simple system that creates phenomenal results in a very short space of time.

It is, in the words of one of my clients, "the closest thing to having a genie in a bottle." I call it The Creation Process™, and it is quite simply going to change your life!

The Creation Process™

This powerful goal-achievement tool is a simple roadmap to having whatever you desire in life, whether it be in the area of health, relationships, or wealth. It involves a series of four steps, which are detailed as follows.

- Define the goal
- Program your mind to achieve it
- Maintain momentum
- Review your progress

Define the Goal

In order to take advantage of the full resources of your mind, it's important that you are clear about what it is you wish to create.

For a goal to be achievable you will need to develop a specific written objective that has the following elements:

- **Word your goal as if it has already been achieved**

Because the mind takes everything you say or think literally it's important to state all goals as if they have already been achieved.

When you begin a goal statement with "I will", you cause it to be seen by your mind as something that will happen in the future. Your mind will do its utmost to fulfil your request and keep that goal in the **future** and out of your reach.

How many times have you used the phrase "I will do it tomorrow"? Have you ever noticed how that turns into next week, next month, or even next year?

To avoid this tendency, always word your goals as if they already exist in your present reality.

Wrong

I will work out at the gym three times per week.

Right

I now work out at the gym three times per week.

- **Include only what you wish to create**

It is very important that you create goals that focus only on what you desire and not what you are trying to avoid.

The reason for this is that you communicate with your mind primarily through the use of pictures and images. For instance, for the next five seconds I do not want you to think about clowns with big red noses.

Now what is the picture that just passed through your mind?

This is the reason you put in the goal statement only what you wish to achieve, as the mind will always focus on the pictures rather than your intentions.

Another example of this is when you're carrying a delicate object and you think to yourself, "Don't drop it." Inevitably, when you think in this way you tend to do the very thing you are trying to avoid.

By including only what you wish to achieve in the goal you are sending a clear instruction to your mind about what it is you wish to create.

Wrong

I am no longer struggling to pay off my credit card debts.

Right

I have now cleared all outstanding balances on my credit cards.

- **Be specific**

Another interesting thing about the mind is that it works best when dealing with specifics. Vague goals of any kind will usually be ignored, as they are not measurable in any way.

Surprisingly this is one mistake many people continue to make when setting goals, and consequently they end up experiencing one failure after another.

If you truly wish to "get there" it's vitally important that you first establish where your "there" is. It's not enough to say you wish to lose weight, get a better job, drive a new car, or meet someone special. You must clarify your goal by focusing on the specifics of what you truly want and filling in the details.

Wrong

I now live in a larger home.

Right

I now live in a beautiful house with five bedrooms, parking for three cars, and two acres of land.

- **Don't try to figure out the "how"**

When setting your goal leave out what you think you will have to do in order to achieve it. This is a common mistake; the reason for this is simple and it's called **fear.**

You may become a little anxious as soon as you start to even think of your goal, which is natural, especially if it means you will have to move out of your comfort zone.

This anxiety often triggers a series of thoughts that focus on how a goal will be achieved. This takes the emphasis off the goal itself and for many people it becomes an internal dialogue that often ends in confusion and frustration.

Trying to figure out how to achieve a goal before you are clear on what you wish to achieve is like trying to cook a meal before deciding on what you want to eat; quite frankly, it is a recipe for disaster.

In order to achieve anything in life all you really need to do is simply **decide** on what it is you wish to create. Once you have made that decision and applied the process outlined in this chapter, your mind will go to work on figuring out the "how" part of the equation.

Wrong

I will reduce my weight from 195 pounds to 175 pounds by exercising four times per week, eating a maximum of 1800 calories, taking three supplements, and drinking two litres of water per day.

Right

I now weigh 175 pounds with 8% body fat.

- **Focus on a single goal in each statement**

Keep your goal focused on a single area of your life. This makes it easier for you to maintain your focus on what you wish to achieve and, again, makes the goal much more specific.

People sometimes try to cram everything into "one" goal because of the mistaken belief that there is so much going wrong in their lives they need to fix everything.

I have often made this mistake myself and discovered that it serves only to confuse the mind and that it eventually leads to disappointment and more failure.

You will learn that by setting and achieving specific goals other areas of your life will gradually start to resolve themselves without your intervention.

As if by magic, your life will start to transform as your self-belief and optimism increase with each new success.

Wrong

I now have a wonderful new job that pays me $80,000 per year, which allows me to afford a $250,000 home, together with a brand new BMW my new girlfriend adores.

Right

I now have a new job I enjoy that pays me $80,000 per year.

There are sample goals available at the end of this book that you are free to use; however, please feel free to create brand new goals while adhering to the goal-setting steps outlined here.

Program Your Mind to Achieve It

Now that you have written a goal on paper that fulfils all the requirements of a clear objective, you are ready to use an incredibly powerful process to make your goal a reality.

We will use the goal statement to stir up all the opposing beliefs that lie dormant in your unconscious that may prevent you from making your goal a reality.

For example let's say your goal is:

"I now earn $75,000 per year."

If you repeat the goal to yourself as if it has already been achieved and then ask yourself whether you believe it to be true, you will force the unconscious part of your mind to look for evidence of this.

As the goal is not yet a reality your unconscious will of course respond to your question with a resounding **"No."**

Your answer will also be associated with a feeling in your chest or stomach area; this emotional energy represents **all** the unconscious beliefs that conflict with your goal statement.

If you were to erase this emotional energy, a significant shift would occur within you; all the doubts and anxieties relating to your goal would disappear and in their place would emerge strong feeling of certainty that it has **already been achieved**.

As your unconscious mind no longer contains any beliefs or ideas that conflict with your goal statement, it will have no alternative but to accept your goal **as the truth**.

By accepting this new goal as something you have already achieved, the unconscious, with a processing capability of up to ten million times that of your conscious mind, will then go to work to make this belief a reality.

In one process you have jumped from trying figure out how to achieve the goal to actually accepting it as something that already exists in your present life. As incredible as it may sound, this entire process can be achieved in less than ten minutes by applying another variation of The Conscious Enquiry Technique™.

The steps to programming your goal

Step 1: Affirm the goal

Read the goal statement to yourself.

Example:

I now earn $75,000 per year.

Step 2: Ask yourself: Do I believe this statement?

If you responded with a "no" then allow yourself to notice the energy that accompanies your answer and proceed to the next step.

Step 3: Apply the Conscious Enquiry Technique™

In this step use CE to erase the energy that represents all the unconscious beliefs that conflict with your goal statement.

After completing this process, you may start to get brilliant new ideas and insights relating to how you can make your goal a reality. You may also notice subtle changes in your behaviour as you start to do things that move you in the direction of your goal, as if you were being guided by some external power.

Do not be alarmed, as this is just the incredible power of the unconscious mind at work, directing your thoughts, feelings, and behaviour from behind the scenes.

Surprisingly, you may even perceive your goal as something that is not really as important as you once thought, and then notice in the following days or weeks how it just seems to fall into your lap.

Many of my clients are totally amazed at the results they experience after using this simple process; a few of their testimonials can be viewed at:

http://www.youwereborninvincible.com

The implications of using this simple process are immense as it totally does away with having to use complicated techniques such as creative visualization, affirmations, or even hypnosis; this is because it taps into the source of all creation...your beliefs!

Maintain Momentum

One of the curious things you'll notice after you've programmed a goal with the preceding step is that you will enter a focused mental zone where new ideas begin to bubble up into your consciousness and taking action on them becomes effortless.

However, after a few days you may begin to question this new-found state and by doing so invalidate the process as you start to create new limiting beliefs. As a result you will return to your limiting thinking pattern and be forced to repeat the programming process.

To overcome this tendency I've developed an additional process that allows you to stay in this mental zone for as long as you desire. I call it "peaking your state" and it involves using a variation on the Conscious Enquiry Technique™ to summon up the ability to re-experience the peak state you feel just after programming the goal.

This is detailed as follows:

Peaking your state

Step 1: Identify the goal

Once you've programmed a goal and wish to re-experience the peak mental state associated with it, simply identify it and move on to the next step.

Step 2: Apply the Conscious Enquiry Technique™

Now ask the following CE question:

"Where is that ability within me to totally and completely believe (insert goal statement)"

Pause and wait **ten seconds**.

After asking this question you will be mentally and physically taken back to the time when you had just programmed the goal and you will be filled with a feeling of 100% certainty that it has been achieved.

Whilst in this state you can quietly repeat the goal statement to yourself with feeling and conviction. This however is not to be confused with the method of repeating affirmations; in using this process you will be totally convinced of the truth of your goal statement, as opposed to regular affirmations where you're attempting to convince your mind that the statement is true.

It is recommended that you practice being in this state anywhere from one to three times a day, for a minimum of two minutes for each goal; this will allow you to maintain your momentum as you work towards your objective.

Review Your Progress

Even before coming to this stage, many of my clients experience a build-up of momentum that propels them towards their goal with very little effort on their part. Some start to get brilliant new ideas, while others become intuitively drawn to people, events, or places that hold the key to making their dream a reality.

However, to ensure that you take advantage of these new developments and to keep track of where you are, relative to your goals, you may need to monitor your progress.

The progress journal

The purpose of the progress journal is to allow you to identify where you are in relation to your goal at any given time and to help you to easily overcome any obstacles or difficulties that may arise as you move towards your objective.

Journaling on its own is a powerful form of written self-expression. It is the technique of writing down your thoughts and feelings and using that information to gain insights about various aspects of your life.

I have adapted this process to allow you to regularly reflect on your life and to help you to monitor your progress toward the goals you have programmed.

The way you approach journaling is to spend about 30 minutes per week reviewing your progress towards your objectives, paying particular attention to three main areas:

- Current goals
- Obstacles
- Action list

Current goals

At the top of your journal page, detail the three goals that you are currently working on. The purpose of this is to keep your goals at the forefront of your mind when planning your action steps.

Obstacles

Under this heading, simply detail any obstacles that you have become aware of, which you feel may somehow prevent you from achieving any of your top three goals.

Obstacles can be fears or doubts that have surfaced as a result of programming your new goal or problems, such as a lack of knowledge or resources you feel may be required to achieve it. When detailing this information, please keep your entries short and to the point by limiting them to a single sentence.

Once you are clear about the specific obstacles you have identified, break them down into beliefs and use the Conscious Enquiry Technique™ to erase them from your mind.

Action list

Once you have removed the limiting beliefs that relate to your obstacles, you are free to plan your next steps, which you can note in your daily or weekly planner; you will find that taking action and maintaining a clear focus on your objective is incredibly easy.

The progress journal is your failsafe system; it allows you to consistently focus on your goals and in doing so creates a clear path towards achieving them.

Practice Session

In this practice session I would like you to experience the true power of this process for yourself by defining a goal, programming your mind to achieve it, and noticing the changes that occur as a result.

To start I would like you to pick a goal that can be achieved in a relatively short period, anywhere from one to 30 days. It can be anything from finding a new job, eliminating a habit, or improving your performance at work.

If you have any difficulty picking a goal, please review the sample goal list included in the appendix of this book. Once you have chosen a goal to work on simply follow the instructions as detailed below.

Define the Goal

When setting a goal always ensure that it adheres to the following principles:

- **Word your goal as if it has already been achieved**

- **Include only what you wish to create**

- **Be specific**

- **Don't include the "How"**

- **Focus on a single goal in each statement**

Program Your Mind to Achieve It

Step 1: Affirm the goal

Read the goal statement to yourself.

Example: **I now earn $75,000 per year.**

Step 2: Ask yourself: Do I believe this statement?

If you responded with a "no" then allow yourself to notice the energy that accompanies your answer and proceed to the next step.

Step 3: Apply the Conscious Enquiry Technique™

In this step use CE to erase the energy, which represents all the unconscious beliefs that conflict with your goal statement.

A. Experience the energy

Experience the energy you identified in the previous step for **five seconds**.

(You will feel the energy in either your chest or stomach area.)

B. Erase the energy

Ask the following Conscious Enquiry Question:

"Where is that ability within me to erase that energy?"

Pause and wait **ten seconds**.

Repeat steps A and B until the energy is completely erased.

Note: If there is still any energy remaining after repeating steps A and B five times, stop and use the **unblocking procedure,** then start again.

Unblocking Procedure

Step 1: Acknowledge the block

If you experience any difficulty with a particular process, allow yourself to step back and acknowledge that something isn't working.

Step 2: Apply the Conscious Enquiry Technique™

A. Experience the block

Experience the energy behind the block for **five seconds**.

(You will feel the energy in either your chest or stomach area.)

B. Erase the block

Ask the following Conscious Enquiry Question:

"Where is that ability within me to erase that energy?"

Pause and wait **ten seconds**.

Repeat steps A and B until the block is completely erased.

Peaking Your State

Step 1: Identify the goal

Identify a goal that you have already programmed and move on to the next step.

Step 2: Apply the Conscious Enquiry Technique™

Ask the following Conscious Enquiry question:

"Where is that ability within me to totally and completely believe (insert goal statement)?"

Pause and wait **ten seconds**.

Note: If you encounter any difficulty in using this process after three attempts, stop and use the **unblocking procedure,** then start again.

Allow yourself to experience the peak mental state for a minimum of two minutes, three times a day.

Review Your Progress

The next step is to create a plan of action and review it on a regular basis with the help of your progress journal.

The three areas you will focus on are:

- **Current goals**

- **Obstacles**

- **Action list**

Each time you sit down with your journal follow the steps outlined below:

Step 1: Review current goals

Briefly reflect on the goals you have programmed and allow yourself to consider possible action steps you could take to make them a reality.

Step 2: Obstacles

Under this heading detail any problems or obstacles that you believe may prevent you from achieving any of your goals.

Once you have done this, reduce these statements to beliefs and erase them by using Conscious Enquiry.

Step 3: Action steps

After erasing all obstacles and problems from your consciousness, begin detailing action steps you can take to make your goals a reality and then enter these into your diary.

After you have programmed a goal simply notice the ideas and solutions that emerge from the depths of your unconscious mind.

From my own personal experience I can only say that what you may experience will seem miraculous and almost out of this world; however, simply accept what occurs and use it to make your goals a reality.

Only Three Goals

As I said previously, in order to keep your mind focused, work on only three goals at any one time. Ideally, you should have one goal from each of the following areas:

- Health
- Relationships
- Finances

These areas represent the three fundamental aspects of your life; therefore, setting goals in each of them will allow you to gradually bring your life into balance.

By keeping your goals to a small number you will find that you remain focused throughout your day as you implement your action plans.

Also, as soon as you achieve a particular goal, you are free to add a new one to your list.

The Power to Create

The Creation Process™ is a starting point, the foundation upon which you can start creating a completely new life. It is not magic, although at times it may seem magical, nor is it hard work; it is simply a process that allows you to tap into all the resources within you to create the results you desire.

Remember

Everything you have read in this chapter is simply a continuation of the general principle that flows throughout this material, which is:

Simply identify what it is you wish to create in your life and remove the internal obstacles (beliefs) that prevent you from doing so.

In the next chapter we will explore another variation of the Conscious Enquiry Technique™ that will allow you to totally transform how you feel.

CHAPTER

NINE

Change How You Feel In Seconds

*Deep within us all is an infinite universe of experiences
that can be accessed whenever we desire.*

Thirty Seconds to Inner Peace

In this chapter, I will show you an alternative way in which you
can use the Conscious Enquiry Technique™ to alter your
body's physiology.

What this means for you is that after you have completed this
section of the book you will be able to access states such as
deep relaxation, inner peace, and happiness **in under thirty
seconds**.

This simple ability will allow you to completely take charge of
how you feel at any moment.

The key to this process, again, goes back to the principle that
your unconscious mind has stored every single experience you
have ever had since your birth: every moment of triumph,
success, and even instances of deep inner peace and calm.

All of these states can be easily accessed, without your having
to use special breathing techniques or biofeedback equipment.

All that's required is that you simply ask your mind to locate
the state within you and allow it to surface. It sounds almost too
simple, but the best techniques usually are. The specific steps
for doing this are as follows:

The Steps to Accessing Resourceful States

Step 1: Identify

Before accessing any resourceful state, please ensure that you clearly identify the feelings you wish to experience before you begin.

Step 2: Apply the Conscious Enquiry Technique™

A. Accessing the state

The CE question you will use to experience resourceful states differs slightly from previous examples because it focuses on feelings rather than abilities:

"Where is that feeling of (insert state) within me?"

After asking this question pause and wait ten seconds to give your unconscious mind time to seek out the desired state. Once you experience a shift in how you feel, go to the next step.

B. Deepening the state

Although you have gained access to the state it may not be at the level of intensity you want, and hence you will need to use another CE question to deepen it:

"Where is that ability within me to deepen this feeling?"

Again, allow ten seconds for the unconscious to find the answer to your question. Once this has taken place and you experience a deepening of the state you can continue to repeat the question until you have achieved the level of intensity you desire.

This is the complete process for changing how you feel in any moment. It's simple, fast, and extremely effective in transforming your mental and physical states in less than one minute.

A Frame of Reference

As you begin looking at tapping into the resourceful states within you, it will be necessary for you to have some frame of reference so that you can easily identify them when they're present.

There are five resourceful states that we will be working with in this chapter; I purposely kept the number to a minimum so you can easily remember them in emergencies.

- Motivation
- Happiness
- Peace
- Acceptance
- Relaxation

I will now provide a brief explanation of the above states so you are clear on what each state feels like when you access it.

- **Motivation**

The feeling of being focused and highly motivated is sought after by many. It's that state of being passionate and determined that allows you to take consistent action in pursuit of your goals.

People who are highly motivated have a sense of clarity and focus on what they wish to achieve; their purpose is clear.

Motivated people know exactly what they want and why they want it; environmental distractions have little influence over them and they anticipate achieving their goals.

Think of a time when you tapped into such a feeling, when you were so focused and determined you couldn't wait to get up in the morning and you get to where you were going. It doesn't matter if you make it up, as long as you can clearly identify the feelings.

Now focus on that moment for ten seconds.

• **Happiness**

Feelings of happiness are similar to feelings of intense joy and success. Most of the time we postpone feeling this way until something in our external world changes and we have a "reason" to be happy.

This is how many of us have been conditioned to behave. It reminds me of the saying "I'll be happy when I have…" This line is usually finished with the words: "more money", "a successful career", or "a loving family." Sadly, the vast majority of us put off our happiness while we 'wait' for these things to come to us.

Do you remember the time you first fell in love, passed your driving test, received a promotion? What was it like? How did you feel when your favourite team or sporting hero won that championship?

Think of a time in your past when you felt happy and everything in the world felt right just at that moment.

Now focus on that moment for ten seconds.

• **Peace**

Peace, or inner peace, is another very beneficial state that everyone tries to find in one form or another. It is that feeling of calm and stillness we so desperately wish to have in our busy and rushed lives.

Many people spend a great deal of time and energy attempting to find inner peace but often end up more stressed in the process. Again, peace is something you can have right now, at this moment, and it requires no change in your external environment.

Can you recall being on the beach when the sun was about to set and all the cares and concerns of the world were thousands of miles away? A time when your mind was totally quiet and still?

If you are unfortunate enough not to be able to recall such a time, think of a peaceful scene that stirs up these feelings for you.

Now focus on that moment for ten seconds.

• **Acceptance**

You may have the misconception that accepting whatever happens in your present life means you are either giving in or giving up and allowing others to walk all over you.

In the deepest spiritual sense, acceptance is the ability to say "yes" to whatever is happening in your present experience and not resist it. Whenever we resist something that is happening in our lives we prolong its effects.

Acceptance is the feeling you get when you find yourself fighting against the world and for some particular reason you stop and say, "Okay." In that moment you relax and a sense of calm comes over you as you stop struggling and say "yes" to the reality you are experiencing.

Acceptance is indeed a valuable state to have at your command as it allows you to move through the world without struggling against it.

Recall a specific time when you experienced such a feeling and simply allowed the world to be exactly as it is.

Now focus on that moment for ten seconds.

- **Relaxation**

To be able to relax on demand is an invaluable resource with a host of benefits to your health and wellbeing.

Being able to access this while in the midst of a busy and demanding day allows you to keep your head while everyone around you is losing theirs.

Think of a time when you took a well-deserved hot bath and all your cares simply disappeared. Feel the soothing warmth of the water as it melted away the aches and pains of the day.

Or imagine a time you had a relaxing massage and felt so completely relaxed and at ease during the session you drifted into that twilight state between sleep and wakefulness.

Now focus on that moment for ten seconds.

Practice Session

Now that you have a reference point for all the states discussed above, you can summon them at will by using CE.

Again, please do not use this technique while driving or operating any machinery that requires any level of concentration.

What you will experience when you ask the CE questions is a shift of energy; again, some of these may be subtle while others may be quite profound. Do not be alarmed or surprised by this; simply allow yourself to experience it.

For the next few minutes practice being in each of these resourceful states, for about a minute each, and simply enjoy what it feels like to experience them. Please give yourself a minute's rest before accessing subsequent states.

Access Resourceful States

Step 1: Identify

In this step clearly identify the state you wish to experience and your purpose for doing so.

Examples:

- Motivation
- Peace
- Acceptance
- Happiness
- Relaxation

Step 2: Apply the Conscious Enquiry Technique™

A.   Access the state

Ask the following Conscious Enquiry Question:

"Where is that feeling of (**insert state**) within me?"

Pause and wait **ten seconds**.

Once you have gained access to the feeling you wish to experience proceed to the deepening questions.

B.   Deepen the State

Ask the following Conscious Enquiry Question:

"Where is that ability within me to deepen this feeling of (insert state)?"

Pause and wait **ten seconds.**

Once you have felt a deepening of the state you may use the question in this step to deepen the feeling to the level you desire.

Note: If you encounter any difficulty in either step A or B, stop and use the **unblocking procedure** then start again.

Unblocking Procedure

Step 1: Acknowledge the block

If you experience any difficulty with a particular process, allow yourself to step back and acknowledge that something isn't working.

Step 2: Apply the Conscious Enquiry Technique™

A. Experience the block

Experience the energy behind the block for **five seconds.**

(You will feel the energy in either your chest or stomach area.)

B. Erase the block

Ask the following Conscious Enquiry Question:

"Where is that ability within me to erase that energy?"

Pause and wait **ten seconds**.

Repeat steps A and B until the block is completely erased.

This variation of The Conscious Enquiry Technique™ has a variety of applications.

- It summons that feeling of **motivation** before you start a new project
- It allows you to de-stress at any time of the day by dropping into **peace**
- It gives you the power of **acceptance** when you notice you are resisting events or situations in your life
- It transforms your low moods by tapping into that deep joy and feeling of **happiness**
- It helps you to unwind quickly whenever you feel tense or irritated by allowing your body to enjoy the feeling of deep **relaxation**

Remember that all these states can be deepened to the level you desire by repeating the deepening questions.

The length of time you will be able to stay in any of the above states will depend on the particular circumstances in which you apply them.

From both personal experience and the feedback I receive from my clients, I find this can vary from ten minutes to several hours.

It's All Within You

The technique I have shared with you in this chapter is one that will prove to be of great value as you go about your day. You have now discovered the hidden switch that allows you to transform how you feel in any moment.

Accessing resourceful states is really just another way of tapping into the powerful resources within you. As with many of the techniques within this manual you will find that your experiences become deeper and more profound with repeated use.

In the next chapter I will focus on how you can transform your relationships with others by applying the timeless principle of forgiveness.

CHAPTER

TEN

Heal Your Relationships

Forgiveness frees you to live in the present and closes the book on the past.

The Healing Power of Forgiveness

It may seem a little strange to read about overcoming obstacles and achieving your dreams and then come across a chapter on forgiveness.

However, please bear with me, as the principles I am about share with you in this section can have a profound effect on the way you relate to others and even yourself.

It is inevitable that as you go through life you will come across events, people, or situations that cause you to become resentful and angry.

Also, if you are like most human beings, you've probably made your own fair share of mistakes along the way, and may have a few regrets or even a little guilt about your past.

In many ways these experiences help you justify the present condition of your life and keep you stuck in your limiting patterns of behaviour. They may relate to a failed relationship, a difficult boss, or even a tragic mistake you made, and they cause you to waste your energy by holding on to painful emotions that do not serve you.

These feelings are like old wounds you have refused to let heal; as a result they can intensify and develop into serious emotional issues.

You may feel that by forgiving others you will be letting certain individuals off the hook (including yourself), yet by refusing to do so you keep your attention focused on the past and find you are unable to move forward with your life.

Imagine walking around all day continually looking behind you; what do you think would happen? For starters, you would probably bump into things and end up hurting yourself. You would also have no idea in which direction you were heading.

Rather than focus on where you want to go you might continually focus on where you've been and in so doing miss the richness of your present experience.

When you practice forgiveness in your life you reclaim your power and no longer allow the past to control you.

You Can't Forgive Evil People

Those who believe it is impossible to forgive murderers or criminals who have inflicted suffering on others fail to fully understand the true purpose of forgiveness.

True forgiveness allows a victim to recover from their ordeal and put the matter behind them. It is, in its purest form, a totally selfish act that allows a person to heal and become whole again.

This does not mean that a person cannot seek justice for what has occurred; in fact, they will be in a far stronger position to do so as they will be operating from a position of strength.

Many people who have experienced suffering at the hands of others hold on to their pain and use it to fuel their determination to make those responsible answer for their crimes.

However, it is the victim who ends up paying a hefty price for this choice, as they never truly heal, even after the guilty party is brought to justice.

How Do I Forgive?

The act of forgiveness, although often discussed and written about in many religious texts, is actually quite simple and begins with the power of choice.

In order to truly forgive, it is essential that you first make the decision to do so of your own accord; this is not something that can be forced or pressured.

Once you have made the decision to move on with your life and focus your attention on your future rather than on your past you are ready to use the Conscious Enquiry Technique™. This involves a simple process, which is detailed as follows:

How to Access the Power of Forgiveness

Step 1: Identify

To begin, simply identify the person you wish to forgive. This can be anyone who stirs up any negative emotional energy within you, such as a spouse, family member, friend, or even yourself.

Once you have clearly identified the person you wish to work on you are ready to proceed to the next step.

Step 2: Apply the Conscious Enquiry Technique™

A. Experience the emotional energy

You are now going to open up and allow yourself to experience how this person makes you feel. This may result in feelings such as anger, sadness, resentment, or even hate rising to the surface.

Whatever you feel when you think of this person, simply allow yourself to experience it fully for five seconds before you move on to the next step.

B. Access your ability to forgive

In this step you will access your ability to forgive by using the following CE question:

Where is that ability within me to totally forgive <u>insert name?</u>

Once you've asked this question simply pause and allow ten seconds to pass as the unconscious seeks out the ability within you.

As with all the other techniques discussed in this manual you will experience a subtle shift in how you feel within ten seconds. After this has occurred repeat steps A and B until all the negative energy has been replaced with peace.

Please note that it is not necessary for anyone else to be involved in any part of this process; however, if you do feel the need to share the experience with the person you are working on, you are free to do so.

Practice Session

What I would like you to do now is think of a person in your life who has hurt you in some way or who triggers feelings of resentment or anger within you whenever you think of them.

Make the decision to forgive this person **now,** and then follow the steps as directed. If you would prefer not to work on this particular person, feel free to choose someone else.

Access Forgiveness

Step 1: Identify the person you wish to forgive

Think of the person that you wish to forgive, whether it be yourself or someone else.

Step 2: Apply the Conscious Enquiry Technique™

A. Experience the emotional energy

In this step simply allow yourself to experience the emotions or feelings that get stirred up whenever you think of this person; do this for **five seconds**.

(You will feel the energy in either your chest or stomach area.)

B. Access your ability to forgive

Ask the following Conscious Enquiry question:

"Where is that ability within me to totally forgive insert name?"

Pause and wait **ten seconds**.

Repeat steps A and B until you can picture the person you are working on and feel nothing but calm or peace.

Note: If the feelings persist after repeating steps A and B five times, stop and use the **unblocking procedure** before starting again.

Unblocking Procedure

Step 1: Acknowledge the block

If you experience any difficulty with a particular process, allow yourself to step back and acknowledge that something isn't working.

Step 2: Apply the Conscious Enquiry Technique™

A. Experience the block

Experience the energy behind the block for **five seconds**.

(You will feel the energy in either your chest or stomach area.)

B. Erase the block

Ask the following Conscious Enquiry Question:

"Where is that ability within me to erase that energy?"

Pause and wait **ten seconds**.

Repeat steps A and B until the block is completely erased.

After completing this process you will experience a level of inner peace and freedom that will amaze you. This inner peace was always there; it was merely hidden underneath the painful thoughts and feelings you have been holding onto.

Relate with Power

The act of forgiving others and ourselves does not make you weaker, but rather results in the opposite: it frees up inner resources that allow you to make new and empowered choices in your life.

Relationships of all kinds can be improved and healed by applying this process. It doesn't matter whether the person involved is still a part of your life, as the act of forgiveness is an internal process that operates out of the power of choice, which belongs only to you.

This simple application of the Conscious Enquiry Technique™ can totally transform the way in which you relate to others as you begin to experience the inner peace and calm that follows.

In addition to this you will find that people have less influence and power over you and that you are free of the pettiness and anger that formerly plagued so many of your interactions with others.

In the next chapter I will introduce you to probably the most powerful application of the Conscious Enquiry Technique™, which will allow you to heal deep emotional wounds of all kinds.

CHAPTER

ELEVEN

The Power of Love

Love, is the power.

The Long Night

I am a great believer in the concept that everything happens for a reason and in some way it serves us. This belief really hit home after an experience I had a couple of months before the release of this manual.

During most of 2003 I worked on the manuscript for this book, while at the same time building my coaching and training business.

It was a monumental year for me, during which I made tremendous breakthroughs with clients. I also made great leaps in my own personal growth.

However, there was one particular aspect of my life that remained unresolved, something that quietly simmered in the background.

The issue related to a protracted legal case I had initiated, which had been ongoing for the better part of a year.

Up to the point at which I began legal proceedings, I had been largely inexperienced in matters dealing with the legal system. To be quite honest I was a little naive about the whole process.

Nonetheless I believed in the merits of my case and felt very strongly that it should be heard. As the hearing date drew closer, however, I realised I had become a totally different person from the one who had begun the proceedings.

On the first day of the hearing I was cross-examined for about four hours, which was a gruelling experience for me as I was totally unprepared for the type of questioning to which I was subjected.

After the opposing counsel had finished with me, I felt tired and drained and I started to have serious doubts about whether I had any chance of winning my legal battle.

That evening I found myself gripped with growing apprehension about the possibility of losing my case. I was quite surprised by this, as up to that point I had been quite optimistic about the outcome.

The feeling grew stronger as the evening progressed, to the point that I became very tense and anxious. In spite of this, I was able to get to sleep in an attempt to get plenty of rest for the next day.

At around 3:00 a.m. I awoke in a state of near panic, gripped by an intense fear that threatened to overwhelm me. All I could think of was my case and the possibility of a public and humiliating defeat.

It took me an hour with the help of my wife to calm down, and eventually I was able to get back to sleep. When I awakened in the morning I was a little shaken by my experience, which played on my mind throughout the day.

The second day of the case went much better and on the third day I achieved the positive result for which I had hoped, which allowed me to finally put the matter to rest once and for all.

Despite having achieved my victory I didn't feel like celebrating. I was still thinking about my unsettling experience during the night and I was very much in need of some answers.

This incident had forced me to come face-to-face with an aspect of myself I had not been aware even existed. Also it made me realise that there was something missing from the arsenal of techniques I had developed, something I had not anticipated: **How to deal with intense emotional distress.**

I made the decision shortly after this revelation to delay the release of this book until I had both discovered the source of my experience and developed an effective method for resolving it. I felt if I released the manual without this information it would be incomplete and I would be short-changing my readers.

It was roughly a week after the end of my case that I began working on uncovering the cause of my "long night", and as a result I made a startling discovery about myself.

What I Learned

After taking some time out to reflect on this incident, I came to a sudden and somewhat painful realisation.

Out of the blue a mental image of myself flashed through my mind. It related to a time when I was around eighteen years old and made a crucial decision about the direction of my life.

I recalled how as a young man I declared I would do everything in my power to be successful and make something of my life **or die trying**.

I came to this decision after experiencing a year of despair, hopelessness, and depression during which I had many personal struggles and disappointments.

It was a difficult and painful period of my life, which I eventually overcame through seeking knowledge and developing an interest in the area of self-help.

What was crucial to my recovery at the time was the decision to make something of myself **no matter what the cost**; failure as far as I was concerned was no longer an option.

It was this key decision that was the clue to why I became so overwhelmed with fear during my legal case.

After making this discovery I began to realise how much this early decision had been affecting my life, how it had driven me to push myself to my physical and mental limits, which in some cases resulted in stress, overwork, and exhaustion.

At the time that declaration seemed a positive and worthwhile goal. However, as I said earlier, the mind takes everything we say or think literally and will do its best to fulfil all instructions given it.

Another important thing I learned about that long ago promise to myself was the emotional intensity it generated within me. All of our beliefs generate a level of emotional energy within us, but most are barely noticeable.

A few, on the other hand, can be incredibly intense (as in my own example) and these are often related to deeply held beliefs that are connected to our overall purpose in life.

When something in our life conflicts with any of these beliefs we can experience intense emotional states such as anger or fear during which we may find it difficult to think clearly. This may cause us to behave in a way that to others may seem disturbing and totally out of character.

When a person is in this state many techniques and methods of emotional control become totally ineffective.

This is the dilemma in which I found myself: my emotional state became so intense that I was nothing more than a helpless, trembling mess.

My serious concerns about my legal case caused my unconscious beliefs relating to failure to trigger a torrent of intense fear within me. This was due to the fact that losing my case would have been not only a personal failure for me but also a public one: something my belief system would have found impossible to accept.

In the midst of this experience I was incapable of clearly identifying the underlying beliefs that caused my distress, which made it quite impossible to apply many of my own techniques.

The more I thought about it, the more it became clear that I needed to find a solution to this phenomenon and incorporate it into this manual.

What I needed was a method of quickly but permanently eliminating these intense states without knowing or understanding their true causes, something so simple it could be applied with very little thought.

The Solution

It was while I was reading an article about an old spiritual master that I found the answer.

What I discovered was a unique concept, which combined with the Conscious Enquiry Technique™ would allow anyone to heal and resolve any emotional distress, while at the same time permanently dissolving the unconscious beliefs that lay at the root.

The key component in this process is an emotional state most of us know very well. **It's called love.**

Love, the key to happiness, the subject of songs, poems, plays, and movies, that elusive feeling sought by many and quite simply the most powerful force in the universe.

The kind of love I'm talking about here is not the romanticised version so popular in our culture, but rather the deeper unconditional bond that has its roots in many spiritual disciplines.

It's the love that comes from total and complete acceptance and peace, the feeling many of us try so hard to find. It may surprise you to learn that this feeling exists within you at this very moment and that it is a resource you can call upon at any time.

It exists simply because it is part of our true nature as spiritual beings and it comes in a limitless supply.

If you look into the eyes of babies only a few months old you will notice how totally content, peaceful, and loving they are.

They have no need for designer clothes, wealth, or power; they need nothing other than to be fed and kept comfortable.

This is how we all begin our journey in this world, as peaceful loving beings, until we change in later life to accommodate the limiting beliefs we have created about the world around us.

As this occurs, however, we never truly lose our loving peaceful centre. We can't; in fact, it's virtually impossible. The only thing we can ever do is cover it up with a constant flow of thoughts and busy activity.

The way in which we will be applying the Conscious Enquiry Technique™ is by using the powerful energy of love to dissolve any intense emotional pain.

When I first used this process with a few clients and on myself I was amazed at how fast it worked, not only at dissolving the surface emotions, but also their underlying causes.

I found that even though in some instances it was unclear what was causing the intense emotional states in some clients, they all experienced a permanent shift in how they felt. It was almost as if their belief systems had been altered at an unconscious level.

One of the key reasons for this shift in my clients' feelings is that love is another word for **total acceptance**.

Whenever we truly accept something in its entirety, even if it's our anger, fear, or grief, the limiting emotions begin to dissolve as we begin to relinquish our attachment to them. This is the opposite to resisting our limiting emotions, which only strengthens them and prolongs our suffering.

Love truly does have the power to conquer all, and it is a tool you can now apply. What follows is a simple process that will allow you to heal any emotional pain you may currently be experiencing.

How to Permanently Dissolve Emotional Pain

Step 1: Acknowledge

Whenever you become gripped by an intense emotional state it will often be impossible for you to clearly understand or identify the source of your feelings. You may also feel totally overwhelmed by the sheer force of your emotions and find it difficult to sustain any kind of coherent thought.

When this occurs, simply allow yourself to acknowledge what you're feeling; this can involve mentally or verbally admitting to yourself that you feel out of control and/or are in a state of distress.

By acknowledging your feelings you are stepping back from your experience to allow a momentary pause to take place, which will enable you to focus your attention so that you can apply the Conscious Enquiry Technique™.

Step 2: Apply the Conscious Enquiry Technique™

A. Experience the emotional energy

Once you have acknowledged your feelings notice where that emotional energy is located (this will be in either your chest or stomach area), and allow yourself to experience it for five seconds.

B. Transform the emotional energy to love

In this step you are going to use Conscious Enquiry to transform your emotional energy to love. To accomplish this you will ask the following question:

Where is that ability within me to transform this energy to love?

After asking this question, pause and become curious about where that ability is and wait for ten seconds. Once the unconscious has gained access to this ability you will experience a shift in your emotional energy and a reduction in its intensity.

When this has occurred go back to step A and repeat the process until there is no more negative emotional energy and all you feel is peace.

Practice Session

In this practice session I would like you to think of a situation in your present life or from your past that generates intense feelings of depression, anger, fear, or grief. If you have such an example follow the steps outlined below.

Emotional Healing

Step 1: Acknowledge

Whenever you experience any intense emotional state acknowledge the feelings and then proceed to the next step.

Step 2: Apply the Conscious Enquiry Technique™

A. Experience the emotional energy

Allow yourself to experience the intense emotional energy as best you can for **five seconds**.

(You may feel a sensation of energy within your chest or stomach.)

B. Transform the emotional energy to love

Ask the following Conscious Enquiry Question:

"Where is that ability within me to transform this energy to love?"

Pause and wait **ten seconds**.

Repeat steps A and B until all you feel is peace.

Note: If the feelings persist after repeating steps A and B five times, stop and use the **unblocking procedure** before starting again.

Unblocking Procedure

Step 1: Acknowledge the block

If you experience any difficulty with a particular process, allow yourself to step back and acknowledge that something isn't working.

Step 2: Apply the Conscious Enquiry Technique™

A. Experience the block

Experience the energy behind the block for **five seconds**.

(You will feel the energy in either your chest or stomach area.)

B. Erase the block

Ask the following Conscious Enquiry Question:

"Where is that ability within me to erase that energy?"

Pause and wait **ten seconds**.

Repeat steps A and B until the block is completely erased.

Once you have applied this process you should experience a warm feeling of joy together with a deep sense of peace. This varies for each individual and eventually these positive feelings will fade into the background as you return to your normal everyday awareness.

This particular application of the Conscious Enquiry Technique™ is reserved for those rare occasions when you are in the grip of extreme emotional pain and are simply unable to think clearly.

Examples:

- Panic attacks
- Bereavement
- Relationship break-up
- Victim of crime
- Job loss
- Victim of harassment and bullying
- Loneliness
- Intense emotional trauma

This process can be a lifesaver for those times you are facing adversity of the worst kind and you simply don't have time to apply other processes or strategies.

It All Comes Down to Love

It may seem almost wishful thinking and maybe a little "new age" to even suggest that love on its own can accomplish so much, yet the truth is that this process works in a phenomenally powerful way.

In the next chapter we will complete the final part of this unique journey and usher in the beginning of another.

CHAPTER

TWELVE

The Journey Begins

*The path behind you is but a memory, but the path before you is
your destiny.*

The Path Ahead

Well done for having taken this monumental step in your
personal growth and development.

If you've completed all the practice sessions as suggested you
will have experienced a significant shift in how you feel,
together with a new level of self-awareness.

This manual has provided you with powerful new tools that will
enable you to transform any area of your life. This is not
guaranteed, however, as you will now be required to implement
what you have learned.

This is the critical point for many who read books of this kind;
it is the point at which they decide it's time for change and
begin to apply the tools and strategies to the challenges they
face or put the book aside and carry on as normal.

If you feel the tendency to do the latter, remember chapter four,
in which we explored the concept of comfort zones. Be mindful
of this subtle force, as it is an extremely effective tool the mind
uses to keep you from moving forward.

What Have You Learned?

The following is a summary of some the powerful new skills
you have now acquired.

- **Erase any belief in under three minutes**

You have learned a powerful technique that allows you to erase any limiting belief in minutes, which in itself will allow you to take control of any area of your life.

- **Solve any problem; overcome any obstacle**

You now understand the true nature of problems and obstacles and their root causes, and you have learned a method for overcoming them.

- **Achieve any goal**

You now have a powerful tool available to you in the form of the Creation Process™, which will enable you to create results beyond what you presently believe is possible.

- **Access resourceful states**

Inner peace, happiness, and many other beneficial states are now within your reach and can be accessed in seconds. No matter where you are or what you are doing, you can now transform your physiology by simply focusing your attention within.

- **Eliminate any fear from your life**

The emotion of fear is no longer a mystery to you, and you now have the ability to permanently remove any fear from your life.

- **Improve your relationships with forgiveness**

You now have the ability to forgive each and every person who has caused you pain in your life, including yourself. Personal freedom and the chance to move on to a happier more fulfilling future await you.

- **Heal emotional issues with the power of love**

You now have the immense power at your command to heal those broken parts within you with the enduring power of love. The ability to totally transform those aspects of your emotional life and resolve them at the root is yours.

So What's the Next Step?

Surprisingly, as you share the content of this material with others, you will no doubt experience a fair degree of scepticism; however, do not allow this to dissuade you from making full use of everything you have learned so far.

In fact, do not waste your time trying to explain to others what you have experienced, simply begin transforming your life by applying the various tools and techniques to the issues and challenges you face.

As you do this on a consistent basis you will begin to achieve results, which for many will seem impossible, as opportunities and successful outcomes begin to materialise around you.

Do not be concerned with trying to figure out how you have achieved the phenomenal results you have manifested. Simply accept them and move on.

See the Code

Life can at times seem confusing, with the demands on you increasing almost every day. This can cause you to become overwhelmed as you attempt to grapple with the many challenges you face as a human being living in a fast-paced and changing world.

The solution to this is to not even try to tackle the surface problems you face, but to look beyond your problems and difficulties and see past the obvious. Look within yourself and simply notice what is being stirred up inside you in response to what is happening in your world.

Become aware of the **beliefs** that arise within you as a result of the issues and events in your life. See your outer world as simply a reflection of the beliefs and concepts you have created and accept total **responsibility** for them.

Remember

There is nothing to figure out or understand; the only two things you will ever need to do to achieve phenomenal success are:

Simply identify what it is you wish to create in your life and remove the internal obstacles (beliefs) that prevent you from doing so.

Know the Truth

Another important principle I ask you to take from this work is this:

You are the creator of your life!

To accept this principle fully and to assume total and complete responsibility for your experience of life will transform it in ways that will become apparent only in the weeks and months that follow.

It is not enough to simply do this on an intellectual level: it is vitally important that it become a living truth for you that you feel with certainty throughout your being.

Everything in your life begins and ends with **you**: all your successes and failures are yours. It doesn't matter what society, the media, or the government says because in the end you are the source and as such you are the solution.

Start Creating

Creators do not sit in caves waiting for inspiration or assistance; true creators go out into the world and build businesses, communities, and families, and positively contribute to society.

To be fulfilled in life is to create that which brings you the deepest joy and the greatest happiness, which is your true nature.

It's your time to start creating the goals that will give your life purpose and meaning. Do not wait for the right moment. Begin today and never look back!

You Were Born Invincible

When your mother first held you in her arms she was holding a miracle of creation with the infinite potential to achieve greatness.

You are still that miracle; it doesn't matter what adversity you have struggled against, whether you are in poor health, or languishing in poverty.

If you are able to read these words and grasp their full meaning then you can be set free from the bondage of your past and move to the prosperity of your future.

Begin that journey today!

Best of success,
T.D. McKenzie

APPENDIX

Appendix A
Frequently Asked Questions

I don't know what I want as a career. How can this material help me?

Your belief that you don't know what you want is actually the block that prevents you from uncovering your ideal career; therefore, all you need to do is erase this belief from your mind by using the procedure outlined in chapter five. Once you have done this, you will very quickly become aware of professions that would ideally suit you.

Another approach you can take is to simply create a goal using the steps outlined in chapter eight. This will allow you to program your mind to accept the idea that you know what your ideal career is (which, by the way, it already does).

Example:

I have now clearly identified the perfect career for me that fully utilises my unique gifts and talents.

Once your mind fully accepts this goal as the truth it will do its utmost to make it a reality.

How long does it take to learn these techniques?

These techniques are so simple they can be mastered in less than ten minutes; however, in truth there are no "techniques" as such but rather one technique, which can be applied in a variety of ways.

How do I stop procrastinating?

This can be done in several ways:

The first and easiest thing to do is to access a resourceful state such as motivation, as illustrated in chapter nine of your manual. Once you have locked into this state you can intensify it to the point that you feel compelled to do whatever you've been putting off.

Another option is to simply identify the fear-based belief that is causing you to procrastinate and erase it, as detailed in chapter seven.

Alternatively you can program a goal, as detailed in chapter eight, to create a new behaviour pattern that allows you to easily take action.

How do I increase my salary?

This is actually quite easy to do. Once you have decided on the exact amount of money you wish to earn, you can then follow the goal setting steps that I've shared with you and direct your mind to create the results you desire.

Believe it or not, it's that simple!

Why are our beliefs so important?

Beliefs are the beginning of all thoughts, feelings, and behaviours and are the "causes" that create the "effects" in your world.

Everything begins with belief; the rest is just conversation.

What is the Conscious Enquiry Technique™ in a nutshell?

It's simply a technique that allows you to access the untapped potential of the human mind through a unique set of questions.

My father is an alcoholic; could I set a goal to make him drink less?

The tools I've developed cannot be used by one individual to control another. However, it is possible for you to create goals that will allow you to be more persuasive when communicating your concerns to your father and reduce the negative impact his addiction is having on your life.

What happens if I get stuck?

If you encounter any problems with any of the techniques, simply follow the unblocking procedure detailed in chapter five.

This single process will allow you to break through any unconscious resistance that may be preventing you from successfully mastering any of the techniques within this manual.

This material is great, but how do I keep up the momentum?

The answer is quite simple: continue to set new goals in your life and use each achievement as a springboard to your next success.

I'm currently suffering from an illness. Can this material help me?

As I am not a qualified medical practitioner, the law prevents me from giving medical advice or diagnosing any conditions.

Having said that, I believe that the tools I've developed can greatly impact your general health and your body's ability to heal itself.

A good place to start is to first consult your physician about the nature and cause of your particular condition; the vital information you are looking for is the specific cause of your illness, i.e. what is happening within you to create the results you are experiencing.

Once you have this data you can then apply the goal setting tools outlined in chapter eight to create the opposite effect.

By altering your belief system in this way you will be able to affect your body's physiology on a whole new level.

Appendix B
Sample Goals

Health

1. I now weigh a healthy _____.

2. I now wake up every morning at ____ a.m. feeling full of energy and vitality.

3. I now easily manage my time and priorities.

4. I now regularly exercise ___ times per week.

5. I now only desire healthy and nutritious foods.

6. I now easily drink two litres of fresh water every day.

7. I am now (insert opposite of any medical condition).

8. I now have beautiful and healthy skin.

Financial

1. I now earn a net income of $_____ per year.

2. I have now (started/expanded/diversified) my business.

3. I have now successfully paid off all my (credit cards/loans/overdraft).

4. I now easily save (%) of my salary every month.

5. I am now financially independent with a net worth of ($)_____.

6. My investment portfolio is successfully growing at a rate of (%) per annum.

7. I have now successfully increased the profits in my business by (%).

8. I have now increased the turnover of my business by (%).

Relationships

1. I now have a happy and fulfilling relationship with (insert name).

2. I am now totally immune to the behaviour of (insert name).

3. I now easily and effectively communicate with (insert name).

4. I totally trust my partner.

5. I easily make new friends.

6. I have totally forgiven (insert name) for what they have done in the past.

7. I always stand up for myself when others attempt to intimidate me.

8. I have successfully ended my relationship with (insert name).

Appendix C
References

Dr B Klopfer, "*Psychological Variables in Human Cancer*", Journal of Projective Techniques, 1957; 21:331-340

Michael Talbot "*The Holographic Universe*": Harper Collins

Roger Bannister "*The Four Minute Mile*" Lyons Press

Wilder Penfield "*Mystery of the Mind: A Critical Study of Consciousness and the Human brain*": Princeton University Press

Appendix D
Basic Techniques

Erase a Belief

Step 1: Identify the limiting belief

I believe:_____

Step 2: Apply the Conscious Enquiry Technique™

A. Experience the Belief

Experience the energy behind this belief for **five seconds.**

(You will feel the energy in either your chest or stomach area.)

B. Erase the belief

Ask the following Conscious Enquiry Question:

"Where is that ability within me to erase that energy?"

Pause and wait **ten seconds.**

Repeat steps A and B until the belief is erased.

Note: If there is still any energy remaining after repeating steps A and B five times, stop and use the **unblocking procedure,** then start again.

Unblocking Procedure

Step 1: Acknowledge the block

If you experience any difficulty with a particular process, allow yourself to step back and acknowledge that something isn't working.

Step 2: Apply the Conscious Enquiry Technique™

A. Experience the block

Experience the energy behind the block for **five seconds**.

(You will feel the energy in either your chest or stomach area.)

B. Erase the block

Ask the following Conscious Enquiry Question:

"Where is that ability within me to erase that energy?"

Pause and wait **ten seconds**.

Repeat steps A and B until the block is completely erased.

Erase a Problem/Obstacle

Step 1: Identify the problem or obstacle

My problem/obstacle is:_____

Step 2: Apply the Conscious Enquiry Technique™

A.   Experience the belief

Experience the energy behind your belief for **five seconds**.

(You will feel the energy in either your chest or stomach area.)

B.   Erase the belief

Ask the following Conscious Enquiry Question:

"Where is that ability within me to erase that energy?"

Pause and wait **ten seconds**.

Repeat steps A and B until the belief is erased.

Note: If there is still any energy remaining after repeating steps A and B five times, stop and use the **unblocking procedure** and start again.

Erase a Fear

Step 1: Identify the limiting belief

I Believe:_____

Step 2: Apply the Conscious Enquiry Technique™

A. Experience the belief

Experience the energy behind this belief for **five seconds**.

(You will feel the energy in either your chest or stomach area.)

B. Erase the belief

Ask the following Conscious Enquiry Question:

"Where is that ability within me to erase that energy?"

Pause and wait **ten seconds**.

Repeat steps A and B until the belief is erased.

Note: If there is still any energy remaining after repeating steps A and B five times, stop and use the **unblocking procedure** and start again.

Programming a Goal

Step 1: Affirm the goal

Read the goal statement to yourself.

Example: **I now earn $75,000 per year.**

Step 2: Ask yourself: Do I believe this statement?

If you responded with a "no" then allow yourself to notice the energy that accompanies your answer and proceed to the next step.

Step 3: Apply the Conscious Enquiry Technique™

In this step use CE to erase the energy, which represents all the unconscious beliefs that conflict with your goal statement.

A. Experience the energy

Experience the energy you identified in the previous step for **five seconds.**

(You will feel the energy in either your chest or stomach area.)

B. Erase the energy

Ask the following Conscious Enquiry Question:

"Where is that ability within me to erase that energy?"

Pause and wait **ten seconds.**

Repeat steps A and B until the energy is completely erased.

Note: If there is still any energy remaining after repeating steps A and B five times, stop and use the **unblocking procedure,** then start again.

Peaking Your State

Step 1: Identify the goal

Identify a goal that you have already programmed and move on to the next step.

Step 2: Apply the Conscious Enquiry Technique™

Ask the following Conscious Enquiry question:

"Where is that ability within me to totally and completely believe (insert goal statement)?"

Pause and wait **ten seconds**.

Note: If you encounter any difficulty in using this process after three attempts, stop and use the **unblocking procedure,** then start again.

Access Resourceful States

Step 1: Identify

In this step clearly identify the state you wish to experience and your purpose for doing so.

Examples:

- Motivation
- Peace
- Acceptance
- Happiness
- Relaxation

Step 2: Apply the Conscious Enquiry Technique™

A.   Access the state

Ask the following Conscious Enquiry Question:

"Where is that feeling of (**insert state**) within me?"

Pause and wait **ten seconds**.

Once you have gained access to the feeling you wish to experience proceed to the deepening questions.

B.   Deepen the State

Ask the following Conscious Enquiry Question:

"Where is that ability within me to deepen this feeling of (insert state)?"

Pause and wait **ten seconds**.

Once you have felt a deepening of the state you may use the question in this step to deepen the feeling to the level you desire.

Note: If you encounter any difficulty in either step A or B, stop and use the **unblocking procedure** then start again.

Access Forgiveness

Step 1: Identify the person you wish to forgive

Think of the person that you wish to forgive, whether it be yourself or someone else.

Step 2: Apply the Conscious Enquiry Technique™

A. Experience the emotional energy

In this step simply allow yourself to experience the emotions or feelings that get stirred up whenever you think of this person; do this for **five seconds**.

(You will feel the energy in either your chest or stomach area.)

B. Access your ability to forgive

Ask the following Conscious Enquiry question:

"Where is that ability within me to totally forgive <u>insert name</u>?"

Pause and wait **ten seconds**.

Repeat steps A and B until you can picture the person you are working on and feel nothing but calm or peace.

Note: If the feelings persist after repeating steps A and B five times, stop and use the **unblocking procedure** before starting again.

Emotional Healing

Step 1: Acknowledge

Whenever you experience any intense emotional state acknowledge the feelings and then proceed to the next step.

Step 2: Apply the Conscious Enquiry Technique™

A. Experience the emotional energy

Allow yourself to experience the intense emotional energy as best you can for **five seconds**.

(You may feel a sensation of energy within your chest or stomach.)

B. Transform the emotional energy to love

Ask the following Conscious Enquiry Question:

"Where is that ability within me to transform this energy to love?"

Pause and wait **ten seconds**.

Repeat steps A and B until all you feel is peace.

Note: If the feelings persist after repeating steps A and B five times, stop and use the **unblocking procedure** before starting again.

Appendix E
How to Contact the Author

If you are interested in any of the following:

- individual coaching (limited availability),
- attending a McKenzie Mastery Process™ seminar, or
- becoming a licensed trainer/coach,

you can contact me at: http://www.mckenzietraining.com or write to me at:

McKenzie Training
PO Box 88
Harrow
Middlesex
London
United Kingdom
HA2 0WL

Gains from *You Were Born Invincible*

Please use the space below to note your gains from working with this material. If you would like to share those gains with others please send an e-mail to: gains@mckenzietraining.com.

Printed in the United Kingdom
by Lightning Source UK Ltd.
106338UKS00001B/124-129